T0090416

A
TAXSLAVES
MANIFESTO

Kurt Colucci

Order this book online at www.trafford.com
or email orders@trafford.com

Most Trafford titles are also available at major online book retailers.

© Copyright 2011 Kurt Colucci.
All rights reserved. No part of this publication may be reproduced, stored in a retrieval
system, or transmitted, in any form or by any means, electronic, mechanical, photocopying,
recording, or otherwise, without the written prior permission of the author.

Printed in the United States of America.

ISBN: 978-1-4269-4732-2 (sc)
ISBN: 978-1-4269-4733-9 (hc)
ISBN: 978-1-4269-5489-4 (e)

Library of Congress Control Number: 2010916664

Trafford rev. 12/28/2010

 www.trafford.com

North America & international
toll-free: 1 888 232 4444 (USA & Canada)
phone: 250 383 6864 ♦ fax: 812 355 4082

Crystal water turns to dark
Where ere it's presence leaves it's mark
And boiling currents pound like drums
When something wicked this way comes...

A presence dark invades the fair
and gives the horses ample scare
Chaos rains and panic fills the air...

Ill winds mark its fearsome flight,
and autumn branches creak with fright...

The landscape turns to ashen crumbs,
when something wicked this way comes...

-Ray Bradbury

I wrote this book for four main reasons:

_I_

Entitlement has replaced Ambition

Expectation has replaced Exploration

Taxation has become Exploitation

Will Tyranny replace Liberty?...NOT ON MY WATCH!

_II_

I would much rather shed every ounce of blood in my body and
stand up in Heaven with my Creator than to kneel down on this
Earth, bound by shackles, economically enslaved to my government.
Point your finger in the face of Big Government and say:
"Don't tread on us"!

III

America is not simply a piece of land on a map,

America is an idea...

An idea that was born in the minds of oppressed men who lived
under tyranny...

An idea that was achieved through blood during the Revolutionary
War...

And an idea that burns in the hearts and minds of free men and
women on all corners of this earth.

_IV_

The last time I raised my hand over my heart and pledged allegiance
to my flag it was not red, and it did not have a hammer and sickle...
it had the stars and stripes and it was red, white and blue!!
These colors don't run and neither do we.

Contents

INTRODUCTION

I would like to take a moment to explain the reasons why I chose the front and back covers for this book.

The significance of both is important to gain a clear understanding of my motivation for writing this book:

1- Both covers are paintings my Grandfather made, so they have a very special meaning to me. They bring me back to my childhood. I can still imagine them hanging on the walls of my family home. Now, just as then, I smile when I look at them.

2- Both covers represent two very different symbols that represent the best and worst of our natural human characteristics:

Creation and Destruction

FRONT COVER: *CREATION*

Take a good look at the different images on the front cover. All are symbols that represent the great creations of free men. Centered is the Statue of Liberty, which is the catalyst, the symbol of American freedom and independence. It the starting point from which all the other images flow. The massive New York City skyscrapers, the bridge, the construction worker and paperboy are all images from a simpler time long gone. They represent a time of personal responsibility, creation, achievement and self-reliance. These images symbolize what has become our greatest characteristic as Americans - Freedom. The greatest achievement of American Freedom is **CREATION.**

BACK COVER: *DESTRUCTION*

The back cover represents a drastic difference from the front cover, a completely different world. One filled with gloom, hopelessness and despair. As my Grandfather explained, it symbolized the last living creature on earth after nuclear war destroyed civilization- a starving dog. It was painted during the Cold War between the United States of America and former Union of Soviet Socialist Republics. At the time, the looming threat of nuclear destruction was a constantly present reality. Look closely at the image. The dog, starved down to its bare ribs was "walking the plank" to its death - not self-inflicted but self-sacrificing.

This represents the worst of our natural human characteristics- **DESTRUCTION**

You may be wondering what this has to do with taxation, so I will explain. **Taxation has the power to create or destroy our American Nation.**

Between **Creation** (Front Cover) and **Destruction** (Back Cover) lies **Hope** (The pages in between).

The pages in this book represent my hope that we will wake up and return to a time of greater freedom, better sensibility and awaken the creative spirit that dwells deep within each of us as humans, and as Americans.

Which cover will you chose to leave face up on your coffee table, the front or the back?

I would like to remind you that my writing is not meant to be a great literary work of art. It is my intention to keep the words simple and understandable so that the content is written in a way that would be the same as if the words were to come out of my mouth, nothing fancy - just real and from my heart.

I have absolutely no business writing a book on politics or government, but I did anyway. After all, I am an American, and revolution is in my blood.

Don't simply chase your dreams. Instead, hunt them down! I have a dream…and just as Martin Luther King told the world about his dream, I have one of my own. I cannot wait for the day to come when I can loudly proclaim…

Free at Last,

Free at Last,

The American Taxslaves are Free at Last.

We are living in one of the most explosive moments in our history.

This battle is not only political; it is personal.

Stand up and fight for your independence.

I thankfully present to you…

A Taxslaves Manifesto

A disturbing trend is haunting America; Economic Enslavement

The political powers of our land have entered into an unholy alliance. **We have become a society of Taxslaves, entrenched in government dependence; we are now rotting in our acceptance of it.** One thing has resulted from this fact; I have been awakened. The veil has been lifted. Never again will I return to the ignorance of political darkness that once held me captive. It is my obligation to release you, my fellow Taxslaves, from the political spell that has been cast upon us. Make no mistake about it - we are subjects to an elite ruling class. We have been asleep - ripened and fattened to produce an endless supply of ourselves to those whom wish to consume us - and so cleverly do. It is time to take back our destiny as free men, and sovereigns - individual kings. The time has come for us to escape the economic enslavement that has been cast down upon us - like subjects - by the elected "masters" of our political ruling class. The American Taxpayers have become Taxslaves; political prisoners to a ruling class that exerts power and control over "We the People". We have become their subjects. A Taxpayers Revolution has indeed started. If it is not clear, let me make it so; something wicked is coming - the American Taxslaves. We are prepared for a massive uprising and are ready to hunt down the divisive rulers who act as puppet masters. Our goal is to reclaim the right to keep our hard earned economic property and restore America's Constitutional Republic. The legislative shackles that hold us captive will be the fuel for a great release. It is time to break free from this system of Tax

Enslavement and cast out the sinister men of greed who seek to maintain dominion over us. It is now time to launch a new revolutionary battle - a war against Tax Slavery.

An unthinkable presence has once again invaded our shores.
It is time for the American Taxslaves to rise up from politically
enforced economic servitude and reclaim independence.
Refuse to surrender your liberty to the chains of slavery.
Now is the time to rise up and re-write this tale of American
Tyranny. I am here to take back control of my government.

The question is not who is going to let us do it...
The question is...
Who is going to stop us!

If not us who?
If not now when?

These are the questions Ronald Reagan asked at the height of the Cold War. This was a time when America faced her greatest external threat. These United States were locked in a nuclear arms race with the former USSR (Union of Soviet Socialist Republics), also called the Soviet Union. Now, just as then, Americans are energized and hungry for real leadership - not false hope. It seems like our elected and appointed representatives serve no other purpose than to deceive the American public for their own political advancement and greedy self interest.

Our political pulse has flat-lined. If we hope to preserve our American Republic, we must unite together and demand a restoration of government "Of the people, by the people and for the people" within the limits of our Constitutional Republic.

The foundation of our political process was built on trust. As citizens we support and vote for the political candidates that we trust. We cannot allow ourselves to be further reduced to stepping-stones to political power for a ruthlessly ambitious generation of emerging rulers.

Our representatives have become preachers of political poison.

Politicians have become Serpents of Seduction.

Too many of us are satisfied sitting on the sidelines like spectators watching the political contamination of our country unfold before our eyes - unchallenged. Will you sit by and watch the contemptuous reign of our political ruling class while they infect our society with socialist policies and confiscate what is left of our individual liberties? Or, will you rise up and speak out against the political infection and treasonous assault that is being waged against the people of our American Nation? The choice is yours.

"I am not a tool for their use.
I am not a servant of their needs.
I am not a sacrafice on their altars...
I do not surrender my treasures, nor do I share them...
I guard my treasures".

-Ayn Rand

Ask yourself this question: Why, as a free American, should I be forced by my own government to meet the economic demands of my neighbor?

Americans are under the false illusion that they are living in a free society.

We are not free...we are Taxslaves - indentured servants to a political ruling class that manipulates the American people to vote between two heads of the same beast called Tyranny.

Our ambitious rulers are traitors to America. As a result, it is our duty to restore sanity to the political process and stop the growing socialist movement towards a central ruling body in these United States. Just as Thomas Paine did over two centuries ago, once again we find ourselves living in "times that try men's souls".

We are witnessing the birth of a new American Revolution. Our rulers look at us as if we are peasants, in their kingdom, under their rule - here to serve them.

How could we remain loyal to a political ruling class that deceives us over and over again for their own ruthless political advantage?

Stand defiant in the face of forced economic servitude.

Rise up Taxslaves...rip them from their seats of privilege.

Big Government has created a new generation of Americans who actually believe that they are "entitled to" or "owed" a portion of the economic property someone else has earned. (The American Taxslaves have been financially supporting their neighbors - who belong to public employee unions and have partaken in social programs for far too long). Generations of government-manufactured dependants actually believe that it is their birthright to "get" a certain portion of what others earn. Most taxpaying Americans would think this to be absurd if only the strong-armed tactics of our own government did not enforce it.

America's political ruling class has carefully crafted a structure of class warfare among the people in a ruthless attempt to divide us. They understand that "a house divided cannot stand", so we must remember that "United we stand, Divided we fall".

I urge all Americans to Embrace Liberty and Reject Tyranny.

TAXSLAVES UNITE!

A Taxslave's message to our lawless political ruling class:

We refuse to remain government mules bearing the heavy tax burden you have assigned to us...
Our voices will be louder than yours; our hearts will burn with more fiery passion than yours...
Remember, we have been asleep, so we are well rested...
In contrast, you have been working hard to keep us under your spell, and now you have grown tired...
You have failed...
You have been exposed...

This is the beginning of your fall from grace...

We have, at our disposal, the single greatest weapon known to man. It is more powerful than any gun, destroyer ship or bomb that can be dropped on a nation. It has toppled governments and caused empires to crumble. It is a four-letter word, and to politicians it is a dirty word…**VOTE!** This is our **weapon of political destruction!** If you want to live like a free man, I encourage you to break the chains of dependence on our political ruling class. Restore government "Of the people, by the people and for the people". Ignite the flames of political controversy and feed them fuel. The greatest enemy to a free people is excessive government imposed taxation, especially when it reaches the level of our current condition - Economic Enslavement. It is very important to understand that some form of taxation is acceptable and necessary, but not the wealth re-distribution scheme that hard working Americans have been subjected to.

TAXSLAVES UNITE.

We are living in times of unworthy men, disciples of greed, not apostles of progress.

Politicians who serve term after term are out of touch. Like crumbling statues they are relics of a broken past. Taxpayer-subsidized handouts guarantee re-election into office from a voting block of political "clients". This is now accepted and has become "business as usual". What happened to us? What happened to our country? What happened to individual responsibility? What happened to our Republic? The answer is simple; Americans looked the other way.

Make no mistake about it; the reign of the Taxslaves is coming. A political revolution is underway. It has taken root in the hearts and minds of American taxpayers who understand what self-government truly is. Economic enslavement will give way to true freedom soon enough. But first we must fight a peaceful war against our deceptive political class. This is my attempt to tap you on the shoulder and wake you up from this tax-induced nightmare. With a little work we can once again experience the American dream that brave men and women from generations past have sacrificed their lives to preserve. This is not dream of greed and excess, but rather, a dream of independence and freedom - where we get to keep what we earn. To whatever degree you wish to get up and work and sacrifice, you own the result of your hard work. If you fail, you fail. But, the ideal conditions for economic freedom will be yours. First, we must create the conditions necessary to achieve this potential. It will begin when we remove the tax burden that has been forcibly imposed by the political parasites that live off of our hard work.

America is in need of leadership – not political antagonism and masters of manipulation. We do not need politics - we need people. We do not need false prophets leading us around in search of political salvation. Instead, we need men and women of strong character with an unbreakable spirit of determination and ambition who will get the job done. We must re-build the character of our nation. There are people among us who are strong enough to lead with courage, on the front line, proud to direct this Taxslaves Revolution. The solution to the problem of Big Government is all of the regular men and women who want to be left alone to live their lives without unnecessary obstructions. Each of us is a general on the front line in our own local communities. Abusively high taxes at multiple layers of government should be called by the correct name - Political and **Economic Extortion.** It is a full-scale assault on our ability as taxpayers to lead our lives as free men and women - as free Americans. This assault is going on now just as it has been since the beginning of the Progressive movement when we were given the "gift" of a Federal Income Tax. The ballot box is the battleground where our victory will take place. This is the reason why it is important for each of us to awaken our family members, friends and neighbors to the assault on our pocketbooks and wallets. This battle is not about money or materialism; instead it is about our freedom. It is about keeping what you work for. It is about having the freedom to try and fail but still wake up each new day with the hope that maybe with hard work and sacrifice today will be your day.

American Taxslaves are not angry; we are determined. Our generation is facing a leadership crisis. We have a political ruling class that is disconnected from the American taxpayers. "We the People" have become "We the Taxslaves." Why do we accept the current circumstances when we know that we have been reduced to subjects to our political ruling class? America is based on the pretense that the people are the rulers, not the government policy makers. False hope will not free the Taxslaves; it will only further enslave the dependants who rely on the confiscated taxpayer dollars. **A free body of people must work for a living. Citizens must not rely on government extortionists to steal from the "rich" (taxpayers) and give to the "poor" (tax consumers).** Revolution will be our only salvation from political obedience. True leaders will be the people who unite citizens around the idea of what America represents – freedom to live without having to bow down to a ruler. An assault on the American Republic is underway and it is a stain on the sleeve of our Republic. Where is the courage that has been displayed throughout American history? Has it been cloaked in the darkness that has been cast by the political demons in disguise? Has it been sold to the highest bidder? I believe that the answer is no. It lies within us, inactive.

In our own DNA exists the blood of free men and women who have changed the course of the civilized world. Our salvation is red, white, and blue; vibrant with the spirit of people ready to cast out the evil, modern day Tax Tyrants who seek to rule us once again. Our time is now. The rebirth of American freedom is upon us.

Our government did not apply the chains of slavery - we did - through political and legislative ignorance. We failed to take part in our political process. This is about America, not politics. Self-preservation is the most basic of our human instincts. Survival is a product of our desire to exist. Different classes of society will rely on what is within their ability to gain at no cost. Tax Cannibalism is a product of dependence. People do what they know how to do in order to survive. As a human, if your survival is at stake you will sacrifice liberty for survival.

The TEA Party movement that regular American people started has turned into a contagious flame - a burning inferno that is fueled by a strong passion for self-government. Not only did our message spread across the country, but it also let the world know that the shining light of self-government and liberty is still burning bright. At first, the TEA Party movement was mocked. Our political ruling class laughed us at. Now, the world can hear us. We are no longer voiceless fed up American Taxslaves. Our politicians are scrambling because they are nervous. There is nothing they can do about it because the New American Revolution is underway. The American Taxslaves are foot soldiers and generals on the front line.

Let's keep this fire burning bigger, stronger and brighter. We are ready to set this country ablaze with the burning desire for self-government and true freedom. I am ready to bring America back to her glory days. So, please join me.

Our politicians must begin to operate under the "consent of the governed". "We the People" cannot demand handouts. Government cannot effectively direct the course of our lives for us. Voter reform is an absolute necessity. Through this we will change the un-constitutional "new" political structure that is in place. We will once again begin operating within the rules of the political game. Our founding fathers left a road map. Our foundation is solid, but the rules under which our government operates have been skewed. The rules of the game have changed. We must restore common sense and sanity back to a lawless governing body. This will not happen until we are willing to restore common sense and individual responsibility back to the people of this nation. The restoration of the founding movement will take place in our backyards and in our living rooms.

It will not start in Washington and work its way down; instead it will start in our communities and work its way up. We can never again allow our political ruling class, or any political ruling body to gain enough power to enslave us economically or politically. We need to exorcise the evil spirit of Big Government from these United American States. We are free men and women - so start to live like it. There are only a few worthy people serving in our government. As a result, America is in the middle of a downward spiral. This is due to our lack of interest in the political process. It is time for the Taxslaves to launch a full-scale political revolution – a hard-hitting assault on the ruling class we have been forced to serve. Americans need liberty now more than ever. It must start with us - it must start today. I care about the future of this country and the taxpayers who represent the economic backbone of our communities and this nation.

Now is the time to draw the line between Big Government and the American Taxslaves. I am willing to sacrifice my life, every penny and asset that I have in order to secure my freedom. It is my right to live as a free man. If you stand with me I want to hear your voice. If you are against me I want to challenge you. If you do not stand with the Constitution then step aside. If you do not stand with government "Of the people, by the people and for the people" then you need to get out of the way. Wake up! We are Americans; we can still save our freedom and restore our independence. America is not guaranteed; it was earned through blood, sweat and sacrifice. Freedom is yours as long as you work hard to protect it.

Do not depend on any level of government to fulfill your economic needs. It is your responsibility to take care of yourself. If politics and government get in the way, you better stand up and fight.

This is our country and we are not going to give it away.

I will die protecting it before I hand it over without a fight!

The House That Big Government Built

The foundation of dependence is being built around us brick by brick - like a house. The foundation has been poured; bricks are now being stacked up and cemented together. The roof is being constructed, and the doors will soon be installed. The locks will be fastened on and the key will be thrown out. We are slowly becoming trapped in a house of dependence. Before we know it, we will be unable to leave the house that Big Government has built "for" us.

Piece by piece, brick by brick, system by system this prison is being constructed around us. Soon the doors will be locked, and before we know it, we will be trapped in the house of government dependence.

I am ready to take a wrecking ball and knock the house down. We must rebuild it piece by piece in accordance with our Constitution - the ultimate blueprint and the foundation upon which this country was created. We must restore personal responsibility and accountability. I am ready to shrink Big Government down to the size in which it was originally intended to be. Government was meant to fit into a box, and we were the people who had the lock and key - not those in power. It is time to cast out the evil spirits of Big Government.

Let us burn down the house of dependence and set it ablaze with the burning flame of liberty.

"We the People" are the heartbeat of America. So, with that in mind, work hard to be the best you can be. A body cannot fully function with a rotted heart can it? This is why it is so important to understand how vital we are to one another and to our American Nation.

Our movement is not about politics; it is about us - the American Taxslaves - who would much rather be "living" our lives than asking and pleading with our government to allow us to keep more of what we earn. Be self-reliant, and self-dependent. Free people should never plead with their government - free people should demand of their government. We must demand that they leave us alone and allow us to be the best that we can be - not stand in our way. ***"Please let me keep what I earn."*** Those are the words of a slave, not a free man.

I am positively charged and my battery is full. I am ready to breathe some life into my community and my country.

Our current legislators have enrolled our laws in a yoga class. They are stretching, bending and twisting them in every direction to tilt the grace of power to work for them, not the American taxpayers. Our political process was not designed for the select few to partake in. Every single person has the ability to play a part in the political process and political campaigns. Our victory will come in the form of effective "community organizing". We need effective community leaders who are true public servants. It is time to get rid of life-long politicians who bend the rules for their own benefit.

Americans need to get the idea of "politics" off of their minds and replace it with a burning desire to live free and independent from political party loyalty. **This movement is not about the Democrats or Republicans – it is about Americans.** Our country is split into political participators. People on the right think the Republicans and Conservatives will save us. People on the left think Big Government and the Democrats are our saviors. Neither side actually matters. Regardless of the side we choose, they both spend the same amount of money. **Republicans and Democrats are two different heads of the same beast called Tyranny.** Stand on the side of independence. There is an equal amount of political corruption throughout this land of political confusion. We need to get back to the source of the American Dream. We can do this by embracing our independence. Americans must once again become explorers and entrepreneurs. A restoration of American greatness will not happen if we allow ourselves to become entangled and distracted by party politics.

Achievement is the basis of living the American Dream. What is the fundamental characteristic of achievement? It is the creations of citizens who are left to be free and dream of a prosperous future.

Politicians across this land are terrified of the TEA Party movement because it is made up of men and women who have a clear goal - to reduce the size and scope of government. "We the People" refuse to remain Taxslaves. America has once again come alive and the average citizen is working to reduce the size of government. Our rulers have become fearful of losing their power and control over "We the People". They recognize that as our movement grows, the more likely it will be that they will have to give power back to the American people. The American Taxslaves are ready, willing and able to fight this battle. This is a heavyweight fight - not for bragging rights - but more importantly for the soul of America. I expect nothing less from my fellow Americans - we are warriors who are ready to reclaim our throne as the rightful owners of our American Republic.

This is a decisive moment in our history. What we do now will dictate the course of our Republic. I am willing to fight for what I believe in because I refuse to let the conditions that are presented to me dictate the course of my nation's future. I am in control of my own life. As long as I put in the work, and as difficult as the journey might be, I know that I am doing the best that I can for my country – these are my United States.

We are living in a shameful time in our nation's history. Despite the powerful financial and political alliances stacked against us we have a chance to re-establish our American nation. **We must once again baptize ourselves in the flames of liberty.** We will soon witness the return of prosperity - a restoration of liberty and independence. We cannot allow ourselves to be held captive in a state of political turmoil and economic struggle. Failure to take necessary action will allow modern day tyrants to capture the soul of America and hold it hostage. We must win this battle. Our political ruling class is working to break the economic backbone of this country. If the foundation is broken, "We the People" will need to be held up by a government that we do not want and we do not need. **It is our duty as Americans to live our lives free from political oppression.**

We cannot allow ourselves to slip further into a system of class warfare and political control.

This movement must be louder than words.

This insurrection must be solidified with concrete political action.

Inspire Freedom, Reject Dependence

Big Government is producing poverty. In America, we have too many people that are envious of what other people have. Instead of dreaming about what we can do on our own, too many of us are envious of the things that are flashed in front of our eyes - on television, in movies, magazines and newspapers. Glamour has replaced self-reliance. We want all of the best things and we want them "now". But, the problem lies in the fact that we do not want to work for anything. We are envious of what others have because we don't have it. Rather than work for it, we simply want it and demand it. This is not the American way. The American Republic will never survive with this kind of "poisoned" attitude towards achievement.

Reform is needed. No system of government is perfect, but ours is close because our Republic was founded upon the principles of freedom, liberty, and independence. My goal is to inspire people to act. The only effective action will take place in the voting booths. **Control of our government is the only substantial method to achieve our independence.**

Dependence on Big Government has become so entrenched in our society that we cannot imagine our lives any other way. Too many of us give up and fall victim to the destructive idea that government will take care of our needs. I firmly believe that people need help at certain times in their lives. I also believe that it is the role of a community to help people in temporary and unavoidable need – not our government. All of us catch bad breaks from time to time. The problem is, that has become the exception, not the rule. Too many Americans have come to embrace laziness. A terrifying amount of American citizens expect other hard working people to "pick up the tab" for their lethargic lifestyle simply because they do not feel like earning their own way.

We are subjects, living under the rule of a lawless political ruling class. Those among us who speak out in opposition have become the new civil rights activists.

Criticizing government is not hate speech - it is patriotic advocacy. I am a supporter of liberty. I am deeply concerned for my country and I am willing to sacrifice to restore our Republic. Our political ruling class is governing without the consent of the governed. A lawless ruling class is ruling against the laws of the land with contempt.

Why as a free American should you be forced to meet the economic demands of your neighbor? Why would any free person accept a governing body that is deeply entangled in unfair, politically motivated financial commitments? Our "leaders" balance their budgets on the backs of hard working taxpayers that have families of their own to care for. Why would any free man or woman accept the burden placed on them by Big Government? It is because we have been spoon-fed lies. We believe the deception that "it is for a better society". Politicians are stealing our liberty and they are confiscating what we get up and work to earn. It does not take billions and billions of dollars to maintain the needs of a city or state, only an insatiable appetite for political greed.

Productive Americans have become targets. Prosperity is being punished. We are the rightful owners of what we work for - not government and not our neighbors. You are entitled to keep what you earn because you are a free man - not a slave. The government is acting as a barrier between people and opportunity. It is time to put Big Government in a sleeper hold and say "Goodnight"!

Before the TEA party ignited the American Taxslaves- the backbone of this nation- we were voiceless. Now, we are the biggest growing political force in the land. We have become subjects to a political ruling class who have, by their own actions, told us that there is nothing we can do about it. Everything has been set up and designed to tell us that we cannot make a difference. This is not true. We can make a difference. We will restore our economic freedom if we put in the effort it will require. Right now, we are learning how to crawl. But soon, we will be running circles around our ruling class. We are a new generation of Americans who will not accept living as subjects under a ruling body. American Taxslaves want to govern within the confines of the founding principles of our Constitutional Republic. More and more people want to embrace freedom and independence. "We the People" must enforce accountability in government. If we do not jealously protect our liberties, then we deserve everything we get. **Subservience is not in our blood.** A radical revolutionary attitude is what will allow us to restore our American Republic in a peaceful way. First we must remember that our rights are "endowed by our Creator" and not given to us by our government.

A political ruling class does not cast down our rights upon us. Government does not command us - we command government. Liberty and freedom require protection. A free body of people must show a strong backbone in the face of a threat to their liberties.

A free country, made up of independent people who govern themselves must be willing to pay the ultimate price – their lives. There is no room for weakness in a country of free men.

We need courage, discipline and a clear commitment to make the difficult and tough decisions to keep government in its place. Each American must insist on scaling back the size and influence of government.

We have been led on a downward path. Our greatest hope is the emerging citizen activists who are dedicated to rebuild America as our founding fathers intended it to be. These are the people, who do not want to leave anything up to government. Instead these are the people who are ready to serve and pick up the pieces that Big Government left behind. America needs involved citizen activists - not politically involved rulers. Each of us must become politically involved. Too many of us want someone else to do what we need to do. Get involved. Get out and vote. Send a shockwave through Washington and to the rest of the country each Election Day. It is our time to make change a reality, not just a campaign promise.

I would like to know how many of our elected leaders, members of our political ruling class have homes going into foreclosure or cars being repossessed because they cannot pay their bills. Chances are, it is safe to say- none of them - because they know how to balance their own budgets at home. So then, why, when given the public trust of office, are they unable to balance budgets? Year after year they put the public in more and more debt, taking more and more from taxpayers each day. How does this possibly make sense? I don't know who is crazier, the politicians - or – us? I think "We the People" are to blame. After all, we continually re-elect them to office when they have clearly exposed their inability to govern effectively the first time. How can we re-elect people that continue to put us further in debt? Yes indeed, the lunatics are running the asylum. Our legislators more accurately reflect characteristics that are more aligned with deception, dishonesty and scandalous activities than personal responsibility, discipline and accountability.

Politicians encourage dependence, not independence.

They need us to need them.

The productive members of our country (taxpayers) that earn a living in the free market get up and go to work to support their own needs. As a result of high taxes, those of us that pay taxes have become indentured servants to those who do not (tax consumers). I call these people tax consumers. These are people who accept government handouts (social program recipients) and those who earn a check from government (government employees).

At some point we will be forced to tell Big Government that we have had enough. Government must stop stealing our earned income. It is essential to understand that each dollar a government spends is a dollar that has been confiscated from someone who earned it. Government has no wealth of its own, only what is forcibly confiscates from one of its citizens. This is legal extortion. It is up to us - the new American Revolutionaries - to put an end to this nonsense once and for all.

It is time to pick a side. Do you stand on the side of independence and personal accountability? Or, are you in favor of Big Government dependence? Will you allow your government to dictate and govern the course of your life? Most Americans that I know are not ready to give up control of their lives and sink into further economic enslavement in order to satisfy the demands of a ruling class.

Welcome to the Second American Revolution

A revolutionary spirit has infected the soul of America-**The TEA Party.** The TEA Party is a movement "Of the people, by the people and for the people" - not affiliated with a specific political party. It is equivalent to a stick of "Political Dynamite" and it has our political class running for cover. **This is our moment in history. We will not let it pass us by.**

Welcome to the New American Revolution - **we are the resistance.** This is the next logical phase of a progression towards our goal of restoring accountability and true public service to government. This is a movement towards freedom. We have had enough speeches and rallies. Now is the time for action- political action. Legislative power is the only real way to restore government "Of the people, by the people and for the people". **American patriots are once again rising.** We are doing this in the spirit of freedom and independence. **Citizens have been forced into political action, not in a quest for power and riches, or to be rulers, conquerors and controllers, but instead the opposite - a quest to be left alone.** We want to live our lives to the best of our ability without interference from any governing body that seeks to exercise dominion and control over us. This is not an anti-government movement, or simply just an anti-tax movement. This is a movement "Of the people, by the people and for the people". The TEA Party movement took off overnight. **Non-political people have jumped into action because they know something terrible is rotting the soul of America.** This is not a Republican problem, this is not a Democrat problem - this is an American problem. It is not about black or white, rich or poor, young or old. This is not a plan to overthrow our government. It is a movement to restore accountability back to government. The only way we can do it is through legislative power. We must untangle the big ball of political yarn. Our movement is not a hateful movement, it is a movement fueled by a love for liberty and independence. This is a movement towards the warm embrace of freedom. This can be a great moment of triumph, or it can be a moment of great defeat. If we allow our republic to crumble, it will be a stain on the sleeve of world history. Point your finger in the face of Big Government and say, "Don't tread on us."

Martin Luther King said, *"You die the day you stop speaking out against things".*

Do not remain silent!

Many Americans have become conditioned to focus on what they can "get" instead of what they can "earn". We need to remember that "We the People" are the foundation upon which this country and this government were built. Our rights are "endowed by our Creator" and they cannot be voted away by a constituent majority, legislative body, or branch of government.

Of these are "Life, liberty and the pursuit of happiness". We do not live a significant existence without all three of these.

As Americans, we must not allow ourselves to be an oppressed people in the country that a past generation of American Patriots created specially for us. Since the founding era, thousands of men and women have died defending our land and all that it represents. Americans have conquered tyrants, foreign armies, a treacherous countryside and internal conflict. In the process, we created the greatest nation that the world has ever seen. We are "One nation under God, indivisible with liberty and justice for all". I plan to keep it that way.

Our founding fathers ripped this country from the grip of tyranny and I refuse to sit quietly and watch as we give it back to another governing body of political oppressors. It is our duty to protect our United American Republic and preserve the "shining city on a hill" called America. As long as we understand what freedom is and how to maintain it, we will remain "The land of the free and the home of the brave".

Our political system is in need of repair – we must start with drastic cuts in government spending. If we hope to destroy the economic shackles, we must elect leaders who are willing to downsize the huge entitlement programs that were designed to capture the votes of two specific classes of people – **those who do not get up and work,** and **those who work for government**. How can we be expected to preserve a failing political system and avoid social and economic bankruptcy? If taxes keep rising at such a rapid rate, we will lose everything that we have worked hard for.

It is amazing that in America we have people who refuse to work, but still get a portion of other people's hard work. We hear too many arguments in favor of "compassion" and "helping others." But, **where is the "compassion" for the hard working tax payers who get up, work hard and earn their own way – while in the process take time away from their families to do so.** We need our society to be educated, clean and safe, but we do not need groups of lazy citizens who expect handouts just because someone else has something that they do not have. This redistribution of wealth is a full-blown assault on all taxpaying Americans. "We the People" can put this to a quick and abrupt end.

If both the Republicans and Democrats fail to serve the interests of liberty then "We the Taxslaves" will take matters into our own hands and gain legislative power. Our goal is to put people into office that are willing to make the decisions that our elected officials refuse to make. **The fingerprints of both Democrats and Republicans are on the dagger that has been plunged into the economic engine of this country.** We must remember that a government does not create wealth, the American people do. Government confiscates the wealth that is created by individuals only to re-distribute it as they see fit. **Our elected leaders act more like rulers, kings, queens, emperors, and pharos than representatives of the people.**

Americans are once again willing to fight back. Because of this, we are treated like aggressors. **We are not aggressors - we are the resistance.** We are the only safeguards between an over-reaching government and our sovereignty. Our leaders are under the impression that the American taxpayers have endless pockets to support government programs. Our rulers have an unquenchable thirst for our tax dollars.

Our ruling class has become insulated from the economic reality of our times. Politicians and legislators act more like bullies than honest men. Instead of being villainized and portrayed as racists and bigots, TEA Party members should be embraced with open arms. We are the new generation of civil rights activists. Martin Luther King said "Do not judge a man by the color of his skin, but the content of his character." I believe firmly in the truth of his words. **We should not judge a man based on what he has, but instead on his desire to work and sacrifice for what he wants".**

People have come to believe that if you are a "Conservative" or "Republican" or "white" then you are rich. The truth is, we all struggle to pay our taxes. Government sanctioned confiscation of taxpayer dollars is damaging to all of us - no matter what political affiliation, color, race or gender. People also make the assumption that you are "rich" if you own a home. However, in reality most American homeowners are financially over-leveraged. This is why I can say that this is a true civil rights movement. As Americans and TEA Party members alike, we want to keep more of what we earn - simply because we work for it! We believe that we are entitled to keep the ultimate result of our labor – our money. The product of our work does not belong to our government and it definitely does not belong to another person who did not earn it. It is my firm belief that what you earn is yours! Otherwise, you can consider yourself a slave. I do not want to be a slave to government-imposed taxation. I want to live my life like a free man.

Do not trust anyone else to protect your freedom – Do it yourself.

The rulers on the inside of our government are out of control. It does not matter if Republicans or Democrats are in office because they are both equally out of control. Because of this, the American taxpayers are apprehensive about the future of the nation. This is the reason why it is so important to stand up and speak out now - while we still have time to do something about it. Our American Republic is crumbling before our eyes. Are you waiting for someone else to save it? Our founders did not wait. We cannot afford to wait. It will not be a Republican or a Democrat that saves this nation. Instead, it will be you – the previously uninvolved American Taxslaves will save our American Republic.

Ours is a people's movement towards freedom. Theirs is a movement towards disaster and economic enslavement.

Our rulers cannot silence the voice of the Taxslaves. We are the voice of America. Elected leaders have failed to serve the American people. Taxpayers are the economic backbone that fuels this country. We fuel the production and we stimulate this economy. We stand on the shoulders of great Americans that laid the foundation for us. As a result we are responsible for preserving the gifts passed onto us. Each one of us is capable of achieving great things in our time on this Earth.

American history is filled with examples of impractical achievement and courageous exploration. The American desire for prosperity took the original settlers out of comfort to a foreign land that was rich with potential. They made this journey with the hope of a better life. As individuals, we are less evolved and less capable than we were one hundred and fifty years ago. The westward expansion in America solidified the character and soul of our nation. Americans wanted better lives so they went out in search of it - they created a new way of life. In the process, they discovered a level of prosperity and exploration that the people of this world had never imagined. How is it that people with "less" did "more"? Why are so many Americans unable to provide for their own needs? It seems like our nation has lost its soul. Are we a product of our own comfort? Possibly. But, if we want to maintain this level of American comfort and independence, each one of us must make a commitment to become the best that we can be. We do this by making the most of our abilities. As individuals, we must rise above our self-imposed limits.

Now is the time to resurrect the spirit of exploration in your soul. This will only happen when we conquer our fear of failure and re-awaken the quest for achievement that burns inside of us.

We all have a time limit in life. Do not let yours run out before achieving the greatest things you are capable of doing.

In our current political climate, "We the People" are not at the height of our power over our government. Most governments are dangerous to the people because of the simple fact that governments are "…instituted among men." We all know that "rulers" have the capacity to be evil and confiscate the liberties of the people who they are elected to serve.

"We the People" have been reduced to servants who are at the mercy of corrupt Legislative, Executive and Judicial branches of government. **The lunatics are now running the asylum.** Our political rulers interpret the constitution as they see fit. **The American people must once again exert mastery over their government.** Anything less is unacceptable. We must re-gain control of our government. In order to do this we must first regain control of our constitution and the Legislative, Executive and Judicial branches. If we hope to restore our Constitutional Republic, we must act quickly. We can no longer allow our "elected" government to have unlimited "ruling" power over us. Americans must restore stability to the governing process. But first we must begin to govern ourselves effectively. Our actions define who we are and our character is etched into us by our own actions. We must first re-learn how to govern our own lives. Only then will we be able to produce local and national leaders who will bring out the best in each other and in our nation. I hope that we will once again stand united. I know that America's best days are ahead of her.

Relentlessly defend your Liberty.

Our "leaders" have kept the people in a perpetual state of need and dependence

The soul of America has been split into two unequal parts:

Taxpayers and Tax Consumers

We have become so incapable of governing our own lives effectively that we look to government for handouts and bailouts. This is un-American and pathetic. People actually demand that government take care of their families. Why should a government that runs on confiscated tax-dollars be responsible to feed, educate and pay for the children of its citizens? Just as disturbing is the fact that many Americans expect government to care for them in old age. **Where did our sense of individual responsibility go?** We have allowed our society to collapse into a mountain of disgusting dependence. If the economy suffers and you lose your job, or you take a pay cut, you need to make it up by doing something else. Things didn't work out as you planned? Guess what? Learn a new trade or start a new career. If it is not what you went to school for, or in the field that you previously worked in, you can still learn how to do something new. It might take time, sacrifice and hard work, but so what – everything does. You must do what you need to do in order to survive and provide for your family. Even if the pay is low you must remember that there are twenty-four hours in a day, so go out and work hard.

All Americans need to provide for themselves and stop demanding that government provide for them. Government can only do what it has the money to do. The more government must do the more government must confiscate from its taxpaying citizens. How can we expect to lower the cost of government if it is responsible for the "needs" of all of its citizens? Our political rulers have put the working class of Americans on the verge of economic collapse because they made promises in return for votes. In an attempt to secure additional votes, politicians serving in government have more people to educate, more mouths to feed, more unemployed people to support, more people to house and more checks to provide for people who are not earning their own way. This is nothing less than wealth re-distribution - which is unfair and un-constitutional. Wealth re-distribution goes against everything America stands for. As well, it is the driving force behind government enforced economic servitude and Tax Slavery. **Taxpayers work for the needs of a part of our society that does not work to satisfy their own needs.**

People have asked me why I take this fight so seriously. I usually respond by telling them that since most Americans have lost their will to rebel, I try to make up the difference. Although I try, I know I cannot do it alone. I need help. Most Taxslaves refuse to accept their peasant-like conditions. The will of the American Taxslaves is almost broken. Our ruling class if fully aware of this. They know that that their actions are destructive. Sadly, some of the American people have discovered that they can vote themselves money from the people and businesses that earn it. As a result, there is no incentive to go earn a living through achievement and merit.

We are sinking into the Bermuda Triangle of economic ruin.

Thanks to "community organizers" like President Obama, people have voted themselves benefits upon benefits - all at the expense of the taxpaying portion of our country. Because of this, we are losing our economic independence.

It is your duty as an American to keep your finger on the pulse of revolution.

Our tax system is like a variable interest rate - interest rates can go up or down. Taxes only travel one direction - up. This is a problem because it prevents long term financial planning for businesses and individuals. The entire country must rise up against this political abuse. We must fight back against the attempted conquest of the American Taxslaves. Our rulers continue to gain political supremacy and as a result have established economic dominance over us. **"We the People" have been reduced to Taxslaves. Because of our indifference to government policy, we have sentenced ourselves to self-imposed Tax Slavery.** The average American citizen does not need to run for office to make a difference. We need to put in the time to get to know who is running for office, what they stand for and what they intend to do if elected.

This is a quest for freedom from tyranny. My thoughts, feelings, and beliefs are rooted in a strong desire to live free from political and economic oppression.

Why, as a free American, should I be forced, by my own government, to meet the economic demands of my neighbor? If I get up and go to work, I should not have to give my paycheck to another person who does not get up and work as hard, who has half the ambition and work ethic that I do. Why should another person get what you work for just because it is in the best interest of the "community"? I work for what I want, so I should not be forced, by my government, to finance those in this country that are not willing to work and sacrifice to meet their own needs.

Dependence on Big Government is an addiction - a curable sickness. We need to orchestrate an intervention and force ourselves into a political detoxification program. We must become infused with a clear understanding of what it really means to live free. Our lives must be firmly rooted in the concept of self-preservation by way of self-government. **Government must not be used as a tool to provide for us. Instead, government should be a tool used to make sure that individuals can provide for themselves.**

We are blessed each day of our lives. It is a great privilege to wake up every day and count my blessings – I am thankful for being able to call myself an American. The people of our nation have more opportunity to achieve prosperity than any other people that have ever walked this Earth.

Political action will propel us towards greater prosperity. Relentless political activism will get us back on the right track.

Our ruling class treats its subjects (the Taxpayers) like an endless bank account. We must force our elected "leaders" to govern, and spend tax dollars wisely. The simplest way to send a message is to vote unaffordable local budgets down. Government on all levels must begin to work within reasonable budgets. Let them know that the Taxslaves will no longer provide the funding for their reckless appetite for our tax dollars. Let your elected officials know that we will no longer sit back and live as subjects to a lawless political ruling class. Speak out and demand that they begin operating under the "consent of the governed". Every single dollar in every government budget must be spent with careful discipline and cautious restraint.

The easiest way to guarantee failure in our government is to do nothing. If we fail to pay attention and refuse to take political action when necessary by speaking out on issues that will cost the taxpayers more of their earned income, America will sink deeper into the hole of economic oppression. **We must force them to govern**, not allow them to ride on the backs of taxpayers.

Taxation is a tool of Economic Tyranny!

The growing threat of centralized planning by our Federal Government is closing in on us more and more each day. Because of this, the future of America is in danger. We need to find leaders who are passionate and committed to retaining and restoring American greatness. **We must build on the great achievements of the past and work towards a more prosperous future.**

Thanks to the Tea party activists, we are witnessing a re-birth of the Independent American Spirit. **We are in the middle of a political insurrection – an uprising made up of abused American Taxslaves.** "We the People" refuse to remain silent. At a time when our country is facing its greatest challenge from within, the Tea Party movement gives me hope. Not false hope, but real excitement, generated from the American people who want to take back control of their government. I am excited to think that the wave of Big Government that has been building is almost at its breaking point. I hope that I can look back and say that I was one of the many great Americans who contributed to the rebellion that defeated a modern day monarchy. I am ready to restore government "Of the people, by the people and for the people." I hope to make our founding fathers proud.

It sickens me when I turn on the news and see the poisonous antagonism that is cast down upon us by our rulers. We are mocked in favor of a class of people in our society that have their hands out for what we earn. Most people in our political class lack real world business experience, and more importantly have no idea what our Constitution was intended to provide.

Because of this, they are operating from a position of thin credibility. **The false prophets of our political class have become doctors of democracy - rather than revolutionaries of the Republic.**

During the last presidential campaign, our country was impregnated with hope. But, unfortunately "We the People" were just used and abused. Like a victim of seduction, we were told what we wanted to hear. Someone exploited our insecurities and gave us hope - only to let us down. We were willing participants in our own seduction. Although things did not work out as planned, we must move on and learn from our mistakes. **We must now work to resurrect America one Taxslave at a time.** Arm yourselves with knowledge and information, and then spread the word that America is once again rising-up. Our country is under invasion by a lawless political ruling class that is so far out of touch with the average American taxpayer. We have been reduced to Tax Peasants who work for the benefit of a cash thirsty machine called Big Government.

I hold this truth to be self-evident; **our rulers are taxing the life out of us.** Prosperity is being punished. Achievement and financial reward are now prosecuted instead of promoted. This is something to be ashamed of. It is time for us to write our own chapter in American history.

It is time to resurrect the soul of America.

We do not need a new system of government; instead we need to systematically replace those serving in government. We need leaders that are ready to make government operate within the confines of which it was originally intended to function.

This can be achieved by electing true public servants - only then will we be able to eat the monster of Big Government from the inside out. **Election Day is our time to testify against our abusive rulers.** We cannot allow ourselves to be subjects who obey the demands of an imperial governing body. We are in the late rounds of a heavyweight fight and it is time to let our hands fly. **There can be no compromise, no retreat and no surrender.** America is in a battle for her life. The grip of our abusive ruling class is tightening more and more each day.

Election Day will be our chance to cast out the evil spirits within our government just as Lucifer and his fallen angels were cast down from Heaven. It is our duty as Americans to remove every elected official from office who has failed to stand on the side of the American Taxslaves. It is time for us to throw the false prophets out of our government. The words

"Of the people, by the people and for the people" can no longer be words we memorize from a far removed past. Instead, they must be the governing rules by which we hold our leaders accountable. I will not rest until I can loudly proclaim these words in the spirit of Martin Luther King:

"Free at last...

Free at last...

The American Taxslaves are free at last..."

If government keeps stealing from the wealth-creating portion of society, our country will collapse into greater economic despair. The only safeguard we can rely on is ourselves– not those within our government. We cannot depend on our governing bodies to employ us, feed us, educate us, give us homes, clothe us and take care of our needs and wants. This is not the role that our government was meant to serve.

Slaves and prisoners are provided for. They serve a master.

Free men make their own way and are masters of their own lives.

We are watching the dawn of a dreadful era in American politics. Political isolation has removed the average citizen from the roots of this nation – self-government.

We are faced with an internal threat greater than we have ever faced from within. We need to reduce our dependence on government because it is a disease – a dangerous illness that will consume our country unless we destroy it in the early stages.

Men have mastered the art of manipulating politics and as a result - government. In anticipation of this, our founders laid the foundation of our government with a Constitutional Republic. They left us safeguards, intended to curb one of the most prevalent natural tendencies of man… the desire to rule.

Become a prisoner to your own ambition…

It is time to free the American Taxslaves.

We need to work towards the common goal of restoring liberty in America. To do this, we must have a firm understanding of what freedom, independence and ultimately liberty really are. Very few Americans have a true understanding of what our government was originally set up to provide. We need to work hard to learn what the proper role of government is in our lives. Operation under the rule of law is the responsibility of government.

So then, what is the responsibility of the individual? What is government's responsibility to the individual, and what is an individual's responsibility to their government? We can no longer accept a majority rule. If we are not careful, we can be tricked by our misleading political class and vote our way into permanent political and economic enslavement. A dangerous combination of politicians, media outlets, and political investors – through power, money and influence - can force us into Tax Slavery and political destitution. We might do this inadvertently, out of our own free will - without a clear understanding of the impact our actions will have on our own lives. **What is our political destiny?** Is it economic servitude through government nationalization? Or, is it American prosperity by way of free market principles? Government should not make "business" its business.

Economic servitude is being imposed on the working class, taxpaying Americans by voters who are either *employed by government*, *supported by government*, or *indifferent to government*.

We urgently need to get in tune with our political atmosphere.

Americans are once again capable of political enlightenment. All we have to do is open our eyes and look at the people and circumstances around us. American society is being split into two groups - Taxpayers and Tax Consumers. This is a dangerous societal split. Why is one group of the American people responsible for the financial well-being of another group of people? Each one of us has the opportunity to work to the best of our ability, so why don't we? **Why is it that the people who refuse to work hard get the benefits of a government "award program"? Politicians take what working class Americans earn and simply "hand it over" to public employees, social program recipients and voting blocks of people that look to gain an economic advantage at the expense of hard working people?**

Although there is no shortage of American Taxslaves who complain about this gross **political malpractice**, there is a lack of action taken to correct the problem of political thievery. We must remember that **the political destiny of these United States is in the hands of "We the People".** We are watching the self-destruction of America, at the hands of political indifference. Our elected officials have shown that they are unconstrained by law and as a result it is now "open season" on the pockets of the American Taxslaves.

Members of our political class have transformed themselves from "leaders" into "rulers", and as a result, our government has changed from the voice of reason to the voice of treason. It is time for the American Taxslaves to break the shackles that hold us captive. America is facing a political crisis. One like our nation has never seen before. "We the People" have been misled and manipulated by the unjust influence of our ruling class, media, public employee unions and political action groups. Each of these groups exerts their influence for self-serving purposes. Our elected "leaders" serve their own interests. **We have become "game pieces" under their control in their "political board game".**

Homeowners in particular, should be encouraged to protect what they have worked hard to secure. Your home is your life's work – protect it! Property taxes alone have caused hard-working men and women to lose their homes – which is usually an individuals greatest economic asset - and along with it, dignity, respect and a lifetime worth of sacrifice and earnings. Critics of the housing crisis that began in 2008 portrayed the mortgage industry, lenders, banks, hedgers and capitalists as the cannibalistic causes of economic failure. Our politicians cried out; "Ooh, the evils of capitalism"! This is wrong! It should be more accurately described as "The evils of taxation and government regulatory interference".

None other than the political class that caused the failure in the first place framed "Capitalism" as the scapegoat. Big Government, oppressive taxation and an out of control political ruling class are the real culprits. Many homeowners would have been able to make their mortgage payments if their property taxes were not over inflated and out of control. Property owners are subjected to city tax, school district tax, county tax, progressive income tax, sales tax, business tax, indirect tax, tax, tax, tax...it is a tax attack and American taxpayers are the victims. Politicians were major players in the demise of many homeowners and unfortunate families. A huge and out of control government is responsible, but not only on the federal level - although national leaders get the most media coverage. Also responsible are the greedy, favor-tossing politicians that are in our own back yards. Look no further than your local community, your own city hall, and your county\state legislators. These "leaders" have become the ultimate henchmen of evil that take from the taxpayers and re-allocate to the tax consumers.

Even though **I support limited social and public welfare programs**, I also believe that it is wrong to take from the "haves" and give to the "have-nots". My belief is based on the logical idea that free men must keep what they earn or else they cease to be free. We cannot allow "elected" government officials to re-distribute our wealth as they see fit. Social programs have created an entire voting block of government dependents that have become trapped in a system of reliance on government. Forced charity has created a whole class of dependents - tax consumers who benefit from the hard work of those that earn a living. Most tax consumers do not realize that other people actually have to work to earn money to pay taxes. As a result, the American taxpayers have been traumatized. **Prosperity is being punished. In a truly free economy, the people create the prosperity – not the government.**

There are tens of thousands of people who work for the local, county, state and federal layers of government. These people are the biggest consumers of our tax dollars because they have negotiated sweetheart deals. Their salaries, benefits and pensions are out of control. Reform is terribly needed. Taxpaying public sector Americans can achieve this reform by voting for candidates that will introduce legislation designed to outlaw the "legal" confiscation of taxpayer earnings. Look closely and you will see that government on all levels has become big business. I strongly believe that we do need governments, laws, rules, and regulations – but not the corrupt system that our government has evolved into.

Are taxes a necessity? Yes, we need taxes. After all, taxpayers have a vested interest in society and it is in our best interests to have a governing body to handle the basic things that individuals don't want to worry about. It is in our nature as humans to strive for more wealth than we need to satisfy our appetite for ensuring individual long-term survival. This is a form of self-preservation that should not be a function of government. However, governments are made up of men and their natural tendencies are clearly visible.

Government has imposed a cripplingly high amount of direct and indirect taxes on the taxpayers of our country. This has caused Americans to feel a sense of life threatening urgency to remove their grip. As taxpayers, we no longer work to satisfy our own needs and the needs of our families. Instead, a great portion of our daily labor goes towards the needs of others that are "less fortunate" and to those who are employed by government. This work is not voluntary; it is imposed upon us, required by law and enforced by none other than the demonic IRS. I believe government should get out of our way and let "We the People" create our own opportunity. It is not a

Constitutional operation of government to either create opportunity or act as a barrier to opportunity. It is our responsibility to work hard and attempt to reach a new level of achievement with each new generation. Success or failure is not as important as the attempt to become better. We simply need to embrace our duty as Americans, without government intervention on a large scale. I will be satisfied if government keeps the streets clean, makes sure police and firemen are available while keeping the justice system prepared to prosecute and punish criminals. It is not the responsibility of government to create "fair housing" in communities that do not meet "culturally diverse" requirements. Simply stated; "Keep your nose out of our business and your damn hands out of our pockets".

We have become victims of self-imposed ignorance

Government employs armies of white-collar warriors. Their mission is to steal what is ours. Lawyers, accountants, media men and unworthy elected public servants - who are fake and insincere - push their hidden agendas under the disguise of compassion. These political mercenaries have strategically stripped taxpayers of what is rightly ours - our earnings. We must not forget that it takes time and effort to work for a better life. Wealth re-distribution is a direct threat to each American taxpayer. We are ultimately responsible for allowing this type of strong-armed government taxation into our lives. We have been taught that if a stranger comes into our home uninvited we should simply ask them to leave. It is now time to ask the intruders from Big Government to leave. As a taxpaying American, your goal must be greater independence and economic freedom. It is in our best interests to learn about how current issues affect our lives and inform our friends, families, neighbors - and even strangers that we need a limited government that follows the "operating rules" that are outlined in our Constitution. This will serve the best interests of all Americans. Collectively, we must find a realistic point of attack to resolve the problem of ever growing governments - from the local level up to our federal "masters".

The most difficult challenge that I have experienced in my daily battles is the fact that most people are so consumed with trying to earn a living, build a career, finish school, find the love of their life, start a family, raise a family, care for elderly parents and sick family members, make time for friends, change the cat box, feed the dog, pay bills, file taxes and catch a few minutes of Bill O'Reilly before bedtime. Simply put, most people are too busy to even think about politics - let alone devise a plot to oust the evil tax gremlins that make our lives even harder to balance. Like it or not, it is time to take our destiny back from the madmen behind the wheel. Our elected "leaders" are driving us in the wrong direction - down the path of self-destruction. A solution to the problem of Big Government is necessary. We cannot settle for compromise or accept our current political conditions. Continuous criticism and negativity will only lengthen our struggle. We need to come up with positive ideas and implement them for the benefit of all American taxpayers. We must work to free ourselves from the miserable conditions of Tax Slavery.

American taxpayers must keep more of their earnings – this is the true result of freedom and independence. I strongly believe that government should play a limited role in our lives. Most matters should be handled on the state and local level. The role of the Federal Government is clearly defined in our Constitution. The states are the true protectors of individual liberties - not the Federal Government. It is important for us to remember that the Federal Government was created by the states –so if it ever became abusive in its powers it was the duty of the collective states to dissolve the American Union. This is not a suggestion, just a reminder of our duty to prevent the Federal Government from intruding into our lives and pockets in a despotic manner.

Too many different levels of government are stealing the income of hard working American taxpayers. It is time for the American Taxslaves to unite and find a way to bond together for our own sake and financial security. Our lives depend on it. Taxes are only a symptom. The mind - set of our rulers is the problem. We need to stop treating the symptoms and find a cure for the disease of Big Government. **We can no longer attempt to fix the problem by putting a Band-Aid on a broken leg. Band-Aids are for paper cuts. We are near amputees and we need help.** Taxpayers are in trouble. The machinery of Big Government is on top of us and it is not moving. It is time to bring in the Jaws of Life and dismantle the wrecked machine piece by piece. We must then work to rebuild it - stronger, leaner, faster and more effective. It is time to re-educate our communities one Taxslave at a time. We have no choice but to start small. **The Taxslave Revolution will begin at the voting booths.** It is your duty to convince passionate men and women who make a living in the free market to run for local, national and federal office. Start your own political movement with real people; neighbors, friends, family, even the people you chat with on the line at the corner grocery store. Taxpayers must elect other taxpayers to office. I promise, if and more importantly when we do this, our oppressive economic conditions will improve.

We do not need change for the sake of change; we need real change in the form of slashed budgets, fewer handouts, limited regulations, and additional choices for taxpayers who seek more fulfilled lives. I find it bizarre that we live in a time where men have the ability to walk on the Moon, NASA Rover vehicles can land on Mars to transmit photos and live streaming video; but governments across the country cannot balance a budget?

It is in our nature to create what we need to sustain comfort in our lives. We can create new forms of governments that are honest and accountable. First, as taxpayers and voters, we must become community leaders and put time aside to get the ball rolling. It is up to us and only us. TAXSLAVES UNITE.

Will we regain our independence from big business government? I believe the answer to that question rests within our own ability to educate ourselves and assemble in a unified effort. We must campaign for liberty and independence all through the country.

Whether you are a Republican, Democrat, Independent or none of the above, you must work hard to re-create a free society; one that understands the beauty of independence. Our individual liberty is hanging by a thread. **We must all work together to repair the fabric that is America.** Our best days are yet to come. The fight will be difficult. Those in power - the special interest groups, politicians and public employee unions, as well as the social welfare recipients of all races, ages, and colors - will not go down without a fight. Despotism is the opposition to our cause. Corrupt "leaders" will use divisive politics and personal attacks to spoil our movement. These tactics cannot divide us or throw us off the path to economic freedom. It is up to you - the taxpayers - to stay focused and stir up conversation with members of your respective communities. It is essential to explain to friends and family that freedom, independence and self-reliance are the only option for a safe and prosperous future. **Economic enslavement, dependence and reliance on government-forced "extortion" are not acceptable in a free society.** Our current "leaders" are so concerned with re-election that they are more focused on being politically correct than they are with doing what is right. Politicians no longer work to protect the individual and economic freedom that is necessary to maintain a free society. **The extortion of taxpayer earnings must be put to an end.** Americans are the keepers of the flame that is liberty. The political winds have become very turbulent and the flame of liberty is now in danger of being extinguished. We must huddle together and create an impenetrable wall in order to protect the fire of freedom. Taxpayers must unite. **We cannot fall further into economic servitude without a fight.** It is essential that taxpayers - the economic backbone of this country - steer clear of blind political party loyalty. Our priorities must be aligned on the side of freedom and limited, accountable layers of government. This must apply to all levels from the local level up to the state level and all the way on up to the federal level. Our government belongs to us. We are our own government. It is time to realize that "We the People" are the true rulers of our own lives.

The American taxpayers must pledge unyielding allegiance to the Constitution and relentlessly fight for the right to maintain independence from an intrusive government on any and all levels. It is the responsibility of our generation to maintain the principles of freedom that have been passed down to us from generations of patriots who have sacrificed their efforts and blood for the cause of American liberty. Just as in previous generations, we will have to face an immense force that will cast upon us a plague of lies, corruption, political strength, and negative press. Our opposition is well funded and prepared for battle. In the face of this, we must refuse to give up our position. **There can be no surrender and no compromise - only complete freedom from political and economic oppression.** We must destroy corruption in all layers of government.

At one point in our history, the states were sovereign (independent) from each other. The individual States decided to unite and create a Federal Government made up of the individual, sovereign states. The Federal Union was created with the Constitution and included a Bill of Rights with three separate but equal branches of government designed to protect the people from a potentially abusive central power. Each state reserved the right to withdraw from the union if it so desired. At that point, each state maintained its own constitution, which was to override that of the Federal Government in most instances. Fast-forward to the inclusion of the Supremacy Clause, which was written into Article IV of the Constitution -it essentially made Federal rule the law of the land – with the help of an activist Judiciary. America was once a free land made up of independent, self-governing states- -and yes; Babe Ruth was once the home run king of baseball.

Alexander Hamilton (a Federalist) stated the following:

"We (states) may safely rely on the ...state legislatures to erect barriers against encroachments of the national authority".

Here we have clear evidence **that a Federalist understood and outlined the importance of states rights. Earlier I asked the question "What happened to us"? The answer is clear; we fell asleep, and as a result, American liberty has paid the price for our failures.**

I am not afraid to say that taxpayers have become cowards. I was taught that anything worth having is worth fighting for. The freedom to keep a fair portion of my earnings is worth my effort. As Thomas Paine said, we are indeed "living in times that try men's souls". What are you prepared to do about it?

We are indeed living in a land of political confusion. This is evident in the words of Vice President Joe Biden when in 2008 said it would be "Patriotic" for people to pay more taxes. Not only did the statement try my soul, but also it severely pressed my patience with government officials like him who vote to legally confiscate our earnings in order to fund their Big Government entitlement programs. The American soldiers who stormed the beach at Normandy under heavy German fire were patriotic. Are we now supposed to believe that paying over inflated taxes to fund the voting machine behind Big Government is patriotic? Paying abusive tax is not "patriotic". The proper word for that is "pathetic". This is **forced economic enslavement through indentured servitude.** We are only as good as the things that we do, so with that said, we can do more than just be expected to "fork over the cash".

This is the reason why I am committed to fight for my economic freedom and independence from the Tax Terrorists in Big Government. Are you willing to join me? Are you willing to put in the time and do what it takes to educate yourself and work to get the attention of your friends, neighbors and family? If not, why? Are you waiting for it to magically happen on its own? Are you part of the problem? I believe you may possibly be. It is time to fix that problem. Unfortunately there is a situation we must tend to, so roll up your sleeves and get to work. We are at the point of no return. The choices that we make today will have a severe impact on the future course of our lives. We are faced with two differing courses of action. One choice is to sit on the sidelines and allow others to direct the course of your political and economic future. The alternative choice is to thrust yourself into political action - grab control of the wheel and steer yourself down the path of self-reliance, personal accountability, economic freedom and financial independence. It will take time to prepare yourself for this, but it is your choice. **I refuse to let our journey as a Free and Independent American Nation come to an end in my lifetime.** We must navigate our own course in the turbulent ocean of political and economic turmoil we are drowning in.

Do not allow yourself to sit back and wait for someone else to stand up and do the things that you need to do to preserve your independence. The battle to restore freedom will be a conflict filled with obstructions. **Our journey back to the Founding Principles will be an all out battle against the disciples of Tyranny.** Let the light of political and economic freedom be your guiding light at the end of the tunnel. If the American Taxslaves unite and fight together, the Tax Terrorists will fall. You may ask, "Who will we unite against"? The answer is clear, our elected and appointed officials who are spending us into Tax Slavery.

The Federal Government is the biggest consumer of our confiscated tax dollars. It is time to put the tax monster of Big Government in its proper place and resurrect the idea of local power, individual liberty and states rights. **The states must once again be a local barrier to the politically motivated intrusions into our lives.** The states have fallen victim to the tax and spend machine of the Federal Government. Taxpayers must refuse to be held captive by a group of over ambitious rulers and a power hungry political class. It is time to put an end to the abusive reign of unchallenged power that the Federal Government uses to confiscate our earnings. American taxpayers can only accomplish this at the voting booths. People will tell you that we are defenseless to the all powerful influence of Big Government. Their dominance of our hearts and minds is only possible because we act as if we have already been defeated. My response is this: Not me, not my community, not my country, not my liberty, not now, and not ever!

Shortly after the bombing of Pearl Harbor in December 1941, Japanese Admiral Isoroku Yamamoto said, "I fear all we have done is awaken a sleeping giant." I think we all know how that battle ended. Fast forward nearly three quarters of a century later. American taxpayers are now the sleeping giant. The alarm clock is about to ring. It is our responsibility to wake each other up. We must embrace the power of our abused masses and rise up against political oppression and economic enslavement. American taxpayers are the vehicle by which this tax consuming machine of Big Government travels. It is time to step on the brakes and stop the Tax Terrorists dead in their tracks. The voting booth is our battleground. Now, the American Taxslaves are the "Sleeping giant". We must educate ourselves and sacrifice our time and energy to recruit those among us who are capable and strong enough to run for local office. Start working to change your city, town, village and county governments. Next, work on the state and federal levels. We can do this if we coordinate and work together. Do not accept this tax madness. Big Government must be stopped if we hope to once again live free from the **tyranny of taxation.** As we have learned the hard way, **elections have consequences.** Each day we are living with the consequences of past elections. Taxpayers still have the ability to wake up and see things for what they really are – plain wrong. **Although it is not too late, we are getting dangerously close to the final curtain closing on us.** If you choose not to listen you are in trouble. If you choose to turn a blind eye then you are only contributing to the problem. We are in trouble if we continue down the same path. The warning shots have been fired, the casualties are growing. The Day of Political Judgment is coming. It is now time to take a good look at yourself and the people around you. Ask yourselves the question "What have I done to protect my political and economic freedoms"?

Given the urgency of our current political and economic situation, we cannot afford to waste more time. We are in deep trouble. The only person that can save you is you! We only have one chance to protect ourselves. Do not allow the Tax Terrorists of our ruling class to grab hold of our government and apply an even greater stranglehold on our lives, our families, and our future. We are all guilty of allowing this to happen and it is now time for us to become part of the solution. Americans must recognize that Tax Slavery through wealth re-distribution is a threat to our independence. Accept the reality that we have fallen asleep behind the wheel. Now, it is time to start fresh. As I stated earlier in this book, we must educate ourselves on the issues at hand and work tirelessly to resurrect our voices; **we are the political and economic backbone of this country**. The American Taxslaves are the new revolutionaries who must fight for the soul of America. It is our duty as free Americans to put men and women of strong character into office. We must start small at the local level and soon after swell on to the national scene. Each of us must work hard to take back our destiny as a free and independent nation. We must re-gain the freedom to keep what is ours - our earnings. As a free people, we are entitled to keep what we work hard for. Whatever we sacrifice our time and energy to earn must be ours to keep. The various levels of government have not accepted this universal truth and as a result do not operate accordingly. Excessive taxation is the same as stealing. The concept of wealth redistribution is flat out stealing – the equivalent of political bribery. As a kid, I enjoyed the story of Robin Hood, a likeable outlaw, who stole from the rich to give to the poor. It is an entertaining story, but our government playing the role of a Disney character is hands down unacceptable! If I was riding through "Sherwood Forrest" and Robin Hood tried to steal my family's means of survival, you can bet he would have a lot less brain matter and skeletal tissue. I thoroughly exercise my second Amendment right to bear arms.

Recently, the infamous Rev. Jeremiah Wright called America "The land of the greed and the home of the slave". I partially agree, but not because taxpayers want more for an honest day of work as capitalists- but because taxpaying Americans are forced to meet the economic demands of their neighbors. America has indeed become "home of the slave"…the Tax Slave! In regard to his comment "Land of the greed", I do agree. Political dependents want life's necessities, and then some, given to them without working for it and earning what they get. This has become the sign of the times for my generation. It is shameful that some Americans actually believe it is the responsibility our government to take care of its citizens and provide for their needs from the cradle to the grave.

It is hard to believe that as a society, we know more about the lives and activities of celebrities than we know about our own elected officials. Many of us can name the cast of American Idol or Dancing with the Stars, but are unable to name the members of the Supreme Court (the highest court in the land) or our state legislators. Most people cannot even name their own local city council members who live right in their own backyards. We have become a culture that is thoroughly consumed with materialism, beauty and sexiness. All you have to do is turn on your television or drive down Main Street to see that we have become a celebrity-obsessed culture. Why? Is it because celebrities represent sexiness? Freedom and liberty are also beautiful and sexy. Control and obligation are oppressive and ugly. I am willing to bet that most people would find it difficult to name a single person they know who aspires to be trapped in an oppressive and controlling relationship. Please, I ask that you check the listings on E-harmony, Match.com or any other online dating website. Can you find either of the characteristics I just mentioned on the checklist of personality traits you would look for in another person? The answer is NO! So then, I ask; why would we accept it from our government? It is because we do not know any better. We are no longer taught how to think. Instead, we were taught to memorize useless facts.

We have been trapped in generations of abusive taxation. Generations of acceptance have led to our tolerance of this tax madness. Taxpayers are the largest single voting block in the country. **We must forget the divisive political games and free ourselves from the oppressive grip that our masters of taxation have on us.** Educate yourselves and start spreading the word that the current structure of economic enslavement is unacceptable. Many will ask; "What can I do? I'm only one person. What difference can I make?" The answer is simple, start by doing the small things that you are capable of doing. Go have coffee with neighbors, hold meetings among friends and members of your community inside your own living room to discuss the local issues that directly impact your lives. Collectively work to resolve matters on a local level. Perhaps you can host a reading of the Constitution - as a reminder of what free men once created when they were faced with no alternative but tyranny. The founders freed themselves from the hands of tyrants - now we must do the same. The American taxpayers must become more politically involved. Not out of leisure, but out of necessity, for survival. **The taxpaying portion of our communities (not the tax consumers) must become the target market for politicians on the campaign trail.**

The evidence is clearly on display for all of us to see. We are overtaxed. Does it mater? Yes it does! Taxpayers must begin to pay attention, not just taxes. Recently, we have witnessed anti-capitalist, Marxist admiring; Socialist radicals stride into the White House. It shocks me to see this happening here in America without greater mainstream resistance. This is evidence that a Marxist storm is indeed brewing here in America. The Communist clouds are coming. We cannot hide out in storm cellars; it is time to face the storm. If we want liberty to survive, we must bear the beating of a difficult fight. Although battered, we will be ready to rebuild our nation. As taxpayers, we are faced with a Tax Tsunami that has been cast down upon us by the self-proclaimed political gods. Our political salvation will come when we elect responsible taxpaying individuals to represent our desire for freedom and independence. But first it must start with us as individuals. I see blue skies ahead of us, do you? Indeed, these are times that try the souls of the American Taxslaves.

Americans are treading in perilously treacherous waters. Our country has drifted with the political current and now we are far from the safety of the shores of liberty without a lifejacket. We are in trouble, but not yet helpless. Instead of waiting for a lifeguard to come save us, we must learn to swim. We must rely on our own arms, legs, hands and feet to get us back to shore. Americans are the only lifeguards of independence - the only savior left for American liberty. It is time to do things the good old fashioned way; put in the hard work to get back to where we need to be; safe and free... the "beacon of hope" that so many have longed to join. First, America must wake up. **Government taxation is a repressive tool used by an oppressive master.** Taxpayers better start to make some noise. The Tea Party movement is not enough. We need to take concrete action and put other taxpayers into office and gain legislative power. We need men and women regardless of color, gender, religions or professions to stand against the career politicians who feed off of "We the Taxslaves". Get out and find honest, honorable brave individuals that can fight the coming battle. It is our responsibility to stand with them. This battle will be won at the voting booths across the country. Unleash the passion in your heart. Believe in the power of your actions. Once we get this battle over with, we will be able to enjoy the benefits of freedom and independence. We will proudly watch the free market flourish and shine like a bright light upon our dark oppressed world. Americans have failed to maintain their independence from tyranny because we accept the comfort that we wrongly assume is a birthright. It is not. We are not safe only because we are Americans - we have become targets. This is the reason why we must be tough, educated and uncompromising in our desire to accept nothing less than the truth from our political ruling class.

We are living in a time where few things are "real". Phony men, women, employers, employees, neighbors, media outlets and politicians surround us. Our world has become a land of make believe. Reality television has become a manufactured product designed to sell commercials and advertising space. That is perfectly fine; I am fully in favor of businesses making a dollar. This is our fault. We blame television stations and advertisers, it is not their fault, they have a right to earn a living too. Good for them if their shows and products sell. It is our fault; we are the suckers who watch reality television shows and act as if they are "real". We are so starved to have something real in our lives that we sink our teeth into misrepresentations. We allow ourselves to be fooled by "reality television". Trust me I enjoy these shows just as much as the next person, but we need to remember it is not real, it is "television". We watch fabricated characters that are so dysfunctional we actually feel good about ourselves. Just watch one episode of MTV's "Jersey Shore", and then tell me you do not feel like you can perform brain surgery afterwards. Do you honestly think "Survivor" accurately represents what life would be like on a deserted island? I think Gilligan's Island is more believable, at least Gilligan did not look like an Abercrombie model running around topless with his six pack abs exposed wearing a bandanna on his head claiming to be "one with nature". This is not real, it is as un-real as it gets. This is fine to watch, as long as you can draw the line between "reality" and "fabricated" reality. I think the most realistic reality show I've watched is "Fear Factor". It is sickening to see just how far some people will go to get a little face time on television. The contestants have consumed blended roaches, live spiders that bite back, huge beetles and cow unmentionables! Now that is what I call reality - people attempting anything for a quick chance at fame and fortune. What has happened to us? We have become infatuated with things that do not matter. We have been thrown off course. This is the reason why government has become so out of control. Taxpayers and our society in general have become obsessed with making a "connection" with a false reality. It is now cool to "keep it real". No, that is what you call normal behavior. Once upon a time, speaking your mind was identified as normal human behavior. **We have become so artificial and obsessed with putting on a show of ourselves, that honesty has become uncommon and unrecognizable. Just look at Washington DC, it has become a breeding ground for fabricated reality.**

I would love to watch a reality show that involved politicians. How great would it be to watch them "evolve" from the campaign trail to the legislative meetings? That would be true "reality" TV. Can you imagine actually being able to watch Obama lash out at one of his aides for accidentally spilling coffee on him before a "Hope and Change" rally? Now that's what I call reality. We all know it happens, so let's get a camera and microphone inside all of the back room dealings so that we can get a bird's eye view of "transparent" government in action. American Taxslaves need to make a more human connection with their elected officials. Perhaps a political reality show might just be the way to make it happen.

Most elected officials deny responsibility for the mess that they have created. For example, at the beginning of the 2008 economic collapse, Vice President Joe Biden is on record stating that the nation will be bankrupt if we (as a country) do not spend more money. What? Can you imagine what would happen if you went to a bank and asked for a loan so that you can spend your way out of bankruptcy? Honestly, think about that for a moment. Does that sound crazy to you? How can our vice president suggest this without blinking an eye? As well, I find it very suspicious that two-thirds of the Federal Stimulus money will be spent just before the 2012 Elections. Perhaps maybe I just have not had enough of the Cool-Aid. Drink up Tax Peasants…you are indeed under their spell.

The past few years have been proof positive that we have become a nation of naïve followers. Just like a liquid absorbing paper towel, we absorb the lies. When I take a good look at other taxpayers I cannot help but notice that they actually believe the political lunacy that is spoon-fed to them. Better yet, most people do not believe it, but still do nothing to solve the problem. It is almost surreal, like something right out of a movie. I cannot believe that this is happening in America. I am outraged and if you pay taxes, you should be as well. The Biden "spend more" example is one of the many political lies that go unchallenged. This is only the tip of the iceberg. Blatant lies and misleading falsehoods erupt from the mouths of the career politicians of our political class. Indeed these are times that try our taxpaying souls. Delaying the inevitable is no longer an option. Americans must become energized, educated and involved. Who pays for the tax burden? Taxpayers do! That is a simple fact. Put aside your sympathies and open your eyes to the reality in front of your face – We are Taxslaves. It is time to say, "Enough is enough". We can do much better than this – America must rise to another challenge.

Politicians have us locked in a deep slumber. It is time to open our eyes and wake up. We must preserve our Republic, and our economic freedom. The ability to regain control of our lives rests exclusively within each one of us. There is a growing frustration among the American taxpayers. The damaging effects of oppressive government regulation and tax terrorism have reached a critical level. Do not be a follower and do not be a silent victim. Instead, be a leader. Lead from the front line of the war on oppressive taxation. Since congress or the president will not declare war on taxes, each one of us committed Taxslaves must declare war against the Tax Terrorists that have ushered in this tax madness. Each Election Day is a chance to testify against the unlawful abuse of power. American taxpayers have a great deal of work to do. We must educate and arm ourselves with knowledge. It is time to get hard working taxpayers on the election ballots. The war will be fought before Election Day. Get good people elected to local office. Go get signatures, campaign, and hold fundraisers for the people that you trust to serve the Constitution and the best interests of "We the People". The victory will be decided on Election Day, but the war will be won in the months leading up to it. Campaigns and elections have become a joke – it is time to stop laughing and get serious. One man equals one vote no matter what they contribute to society. Our political system has been perverted. The voting blocks have become target markets with a political voting clientele. Unfortunately, politicians have come to believe that they are elected to serve one purpose; to find different ways to spend (waste) taxpayers hard earned money.

I find it appalling that everyone has the ability to vote even weight across the board despite the fact that the taxpayers are the only people paying the bill for the wasteful government spending. We constantly hear candidates tell people "Vote for me and you will get x, y and z…but don't worry, you wont have to pay for it, the rich will…. after all, they can afford to part with their earnings". We are subjected to lies like "It is not you fault, you are less fortunate, you were dealt a bad hand, you are the product of terrible circumstances… it is not your fault…. vote for me and I will make it right". Does this sound familiar? Yes, it sounds like every candidate that runs for office.

This is a bold statement but here it is;

I firmly believe that if you are capable of getting up and going to work and pay your share of taxes but you choose not to, then you should not have the ability to vote. Now, I do not suggest stripping tax consumers of their right to vote forever - only until they choose to become productive, taxpaying members of society.

What do you think the average taxpayer would do if after a 40 to 50 hour week of work, their paycheck was given to someone who did not work to earn it and that this recipient could spend it, as they deemed appropriate? The working taxpayer would resist, right? I think not. This type of wealth redistribution is essentially what government does. Because of this, each taxpaying American should demand to have a vested, influential interest in how the money they earn is spent. Unfortunately, we always hear friends and neighbors say, "I don't get involved in politics". This is the root of the problem. American Taxslaves feel a hopelessness that runs deep enough to enslave us by our own lack of interest and action.

American taxpayers have come to believe the hype and insanity that has been spoon fed to us. **I believe that we were all created equal, but we are not all equally motivated. Some people work harder and sacrifice more than others do and therefore deserve to keep the reward for their additional work efforts.** This is independent of color, race, ethnicity and religion. **Tax extortion through wealth redistribution is insanity in action**. It is a crime (in my opinion only, unfortunately not in reality) to confiscate the earnings of one individual in order to provide for another fully capable adult. **Stealing wealth from a productive member of society and giving it to a less productive member has become the vehicle of choice for securing election and re-election.** At what point does taxation become stealing? The American Taxslaves must recognize this deception and stop it before is spreads further. Do not allow this to become a racial, age or gender issue. We are above divisive behavior. This is a movement to restore our Republic. Regardless of race, ethnicity, age color, height or weight, as taxpayers we have no choice but to bear the burden of a Tax crucifixion. Taxpayers are being persecuted for working hard to earn a better living. If you look a little closer you will realize that the tax burden is a duty that is forced upon taxpayers - not a choice, or a rational decision made from a position of charitable generosity. Instead, taxation it has become a "command" - cast down upon us lowly taxpayers by a political ruling class - the Terrorists of Taxation. In case there is any doubt regarding the founders' position on the redistribution of wealth, this quote might help clear things up:

"To take from one, because it is thought his own industry and that of his father has acquired too much, in order to spare to others who (or whose fathers) have not yet exercised equal industry and skill, is to violate arbitrarily the first principle of association, to guarantee to everyone a free exercise of his industry and the fruits acquired by it".

-Thomas Jefferson

$\mathbf{F}$ree the American Taxslaves

The income tax was first introduced during the Civil War to finance the battle. The Southern States, in fact had a constitutional right to secede from the Union just as the American Colonies opted out of the British Empire. (That is a topic for a whole different discussion. I believe it was an issue based on "State's Rights" and not simply slavery). After the Supreme Court ruled against the income tax and declared it to be unconstitutional, it was once again initiated in 1913 when the 16th Amendment was ratified. This allowed for "constitutional" authority to allow permanent taxation. This cursed Americans with the despotic Federal Income Tax. Upon inception, the income tax was only forced upon the richest one percent of the population. But soon, the limited income tax became "progressive" and spread like a virus. It has now directly enslaved taxpayers and holds us hostage to pay all the other direct and indirect taxes. Can anyone honestly and whole-heartedly argue against the fact that excessive "confiscatory" taxes have a profound and negative impact on our position as free and independent American citizens?

Recall if you will the 8th commandment.

"Thou shall not steal".

As defined by Definition.com, the word *steal* is "to take or appropriate another's property, ideas, etc. without permission, dishonestly or unlawfully especially in a secret or surreptitious manner". When used as a transitive verb it means, "to move or pass stealthily, quietly or gradually without being noticed".

Does this sound eerily familiar to the process by which our rulers levy taxes upon us? Do we punish our legislators for stealing from us? Some religions will chop off the hand(s) of a thief. Mostly all countries, states, religions and cultures issue some form of punishment on a person that is found guilty of stealing something that belongs to another person. As well, stealing can take many shapes - automobile theft, shoplifting, embezzlement, financial fraud, and wealth redistribution by government in the form of oppressive taxation. If you compare the definition of "tax" with that of "steal", you will notice they are irritatingly similar. I will even go so far as to say too close for comfort. Unfortunately for taxpayers, in reality, one of the above is "legal" and the other is not.

I believe that oppressive taxation for the sake of redistribution (public assistance and overpaid public employees) is stealing. Once again I want to make it very clear that I am not an anti-government or anti-tax advocate. I believe that we need government to take care of the necessities that citizens do not want to provide on their own - things like paved roads, street signs, traffic lights, fire and safety services - but at a fair price. I believe in the principles of limited government. I also firmly condemn the process of wealth redistribution. Minimal taxation is acceptable, but too many layers of government with astronomical operating expenses have become detrimental to our country. Public employee unions, foreign aid and wasteful social programs are detrimental to the hard working taxpayers of our once free American Nation. It is possible to argue that taxation and stealing are not the same due to the fact that when something is stolen, the victim gets nothing in return for what is lost. At least taxpayers are provided with different government provided services - right? Ok, good point. Now, let's look into this a little deeper from the perspective of an American Taxslave. Taxes levied by government on income, products and services are forcibly imposed on the working class to serve a purpose; to provide society with basic needs like trade and travel routes, safety services such as police and fire departments and "free" public education. Upon first glance this does not seem like such a bad deal. However, the oppressively high taxes levied on business owners, service providers, property owners and our current progressive personal income tax are weapons used by a political class to fund many other unnecessary services that government has no business providing. Our tax code is an example of wealth re-distribution in action - only it is concealed in a shroud of compassion. **The hard-earned wealth of American Taxpayer's is being forcibly confiscated and handed out to government employees at the city, county, state and federal levels.**

Our earnings are also used to fund countless social programs, foreign aid, government projects like Fannie Mae, Freddie Mac and "too big to fail" bailouts like TARP I and TARP II.

In a clear "political" payoff, Democratic districts have received 200% more TARP money than Republican or Conservative districts. They were "awarded this money in return for votes. If a politician gets more federal money for his\her district, their constituent groups will be happy and re-election is virtually guaranteed. Politics has become a vote buying re-election scheme. Political "payoffs" have become a very big problem because it proves that our liberties are up for sale to the highest bidder. This political manipulation is unfolding before our eyes and we are too stupid to realize it.

It is obvious that taxpayers do not get back the equivalent of what they give out. Most taxpayers are smart enough to understand that school district taxes must be paid in order to finance their local public schools. In most cases, the school taxes represent the largest portion of homeowner's property tax bill. However, a homeowner (taxpayer) cannot legally waive the school portion of their property taxes and instead apply it to the tuition for a private school of their choice. Therefore, homeowners are forced to pay for the education of other people's children (no matter how many they have), but are legally and financially deterred from doing what they feel is best for their own children. Taxpayers retain the right to send their children to private schools of their choice; unfortunately it must be paid out of pocket with no reimbursement. In other words, the cost comes out of taxpayer pockets <u>after</u> the public school tax is paid. How can a truly "free" taxpaying American be forced to finance the public school system every year of homeownership? This proves beyond a reasonable doubt that we are not as "free" as we think we are. **In reality, we have become Taxslaves - Tax Peasants under the rule of illegitimate masters of manipulation.** If my argument does not prove this thus far just read on. Children attend public schools for 13 years, from Kindergarten up to Grade 12. Since this is the case, why do homeowners (with or without children of their own) pay an entire lifetime of school taxes? Why not just pay the years that their children attend school? Better yet, why not give taxpaying homeowners the choice to send their kids to public or private schools based on our own free will? **After all, God granted us free will, so why won't our government?**

If you are a taxpaying member of society, you can "choose" the best course of action for you and your family. However, there is a catch- you must take care of the Tax-Consumers first. Most taxpayers cannot afford to send their children to private school while paying over-inflated school-based property taxes. On the other hand, if we remove the mandatory school taxes that home and property owners are "forced" to pay, most home-owning parents would certainly be able to afford the school of choice for their children. Our political system is broken because our current ruling class is out of touch and politically over-leveraged. We need to restore the structure of a truly free Constitutional Republic. We must rebuild our current system upon the principles of freedom and independence. **Americans cannot accept anything less than a full restoration of accountability back to our government.** The commitments to public employee pensions and unions are breaking the economic backbone of the American Taxslaves across the country. Re-distribution of taxpayer wealth to public employee unions is simply a different form of stealing. We must put an end to the political extortion.

Our current circumstances are an embarrassment to liberty and to our so-called "free" society. I believe that our communities should have public schools and I believe that all children should be provided with an education. However, it must be affordable to the taxpayers. Our school systems can unquestionably operate on a much more cost-effective basis. This is impossible in most places due to hyper-inflated school budgets that result from public employee union contracts and unsustainable pension obligations. School board committees and public school unions hold taxpayers hostage. These well-funded organizations play on our fear that the children will suffer if necessary cuts are made to school budgets. Misled members of our communities have been tricked to believe that school districts should have a blank check to spend as they see fit. The public school system is in need of drastic reform.

American citizens must be able to protect and provide for their own family needs first. Charitable giving will flow freely when people feel a sense of financial security. When people are financially squeezed, they hold back what would otherwise be given out more freely.

Taxpayers have sat quietly in the face of economic enslavement and accepted it. Why? **Why have we sat quietly and obediently accepted this burden like good little Taxslaves?** Like I stated earlier in this book, most taxpayers have become so entangled in their own busy lifestyles that they have lost touch with the "real" political climate. Most of us will not even reveal, let alone openly discuss whom we voted for. Why? Why can't we agree or disagree, or agree to disagree on the issues at hand like mature adults? We have become so protective of ourselves that we are unable to discuss who we vote for. We should be proud to discuss why we chose a specific candidate and defend our reasons for it. The only thing we risk is having a healthy debate about what is best for our communities. Even if we do not agree with each other, at least we can begin the discussion of how and why we each feel a certain way in regard to specific programs and important issues. These are the necessary steps we must take in order to make progress and achieve real community building. Americans need to get to know each other again. We have nothing to lose.

Most of us only focus our attention on politics during election years - primarily only during campaign seasons. Taxpayers watch and read news stories that expose the astronomical amounts of money (tens of millions) spent on political campaigns by politicians, political parties, unions and other special interest groups

The majority of American taxpayers get sick to their stomach when they hear that New York City Mayor Michael Bloomberg spent over One Hundred Million Dollars on his latest re-election campaign. This translated to nearly Two Hundred Dollars per vote. As well, take a look at the 2008 Obama-Clinton democratic primary race. I think the combined amount of money spent in this race could have put an end to world hunger.

Although we cringe when we hear these dollar amounts, it is our own fault. The reason why so much money is spent on political campaigns is simple; their goal is to get our attention. Think about this for a minute. After all, if we were paying attention we would seek out information on the candidates. **Instead, we are spoon fed selected "facts", twisted truths and blatant lies by the masters of political manipulation.**

Political candidates use various forms of media to persuade public opinion. Americans should be doing their own research - looking into the candidate's background, policies, and political goals. We need to find out if they have loyally served the taxpayers and the Constitution. What is their take on individual liberty? **If we put in a little effort we would see right through their fake smiles and misleading campaign advertisements.** They serve the public nothing but lies. We have become a target market in a political advertising game. They show us what we want to see and tell us what we want to hear. This is business as usual with politicians. The American

Taxslaves must safely guard their liberties and their economic property from these out of touch political villains. Why should American taxpayers care about politics and political races? The reason is simple - **Politicians and legislators decide how our earned income is spent. They tax and they spend. They decide what programs to fund and who gets to benefit from your confiscated earnings. Government has become a broker of greed. Politicians are middlemen who control the amount of your income that you get to keep. Government does not have wealth and money of its own. It only has what it forcibly confiscates from taxpaying Americans who work hard for their earnings. The more they take the more we must sacrifice. We are not free. We are slaves... Taxslaves.**

Most American taxpayers would not allow a complete stranger to take their weekly paycheck and spend it as they see fit - even if the stranger "promised" it would be in the earners best interest. Taxpayers allow many layers of a faceless government to do this very thing. If you have not caught on yet, just look at the withholdings section of your next paycheck – assuming that you still have a job and a paycheck.

It is my hope that the ides in this book will be the beginning steps of a Taxslave revolution across these United States. This can only be accomplished by men and women who have enough courage to dedicate the time, energy and effort to help build a better structure of government, - one that resembles our original Constitutional Republic rather than the current "take all and do all" babysitting government that we are currently subjects to.

Make no mistake about my intentions; this is a call to action. Taxpayers must bring radical change to the current system of strong-armed taxation that we have all come to accept as gospel. I intend to fight. My gloves are off...its time to ring the bell.

It is plain to see that our elected officials have become more focused on doing what it takes to get elected\re-elected than with doing what is in the best interests of America. What is the right thing for them to do? Get out of our way so that we can live the financially secure lives that we sacrifice and work hard to realize. We must be able to keep our income for ourselves since we put in the hard work to go out and earn it. Government imposed taxation must be minimized - reduced to a realistic level - not abolished, just drastically cut down to its intended size. The expanding machine of government is growing rapidly with each passing day. Taxpayers have become the "fundraisers" for the wasteful, failing social programs and biased public handouts in return for votes. **The bigger the machine grows, the more fuel in the form of stolen tax dollars will be needed to sustain its ever-growing and insatiable appetite.** Do not let yourself be fooled; this is not a problem exclusive to one specific political party. The problem exists within both major parties - Democrats and Republicans. A thirst for power and dominance is in a man's human nature. "We the People" must be the barrier that protects American freedom.

James Madison, the fourth president of the United States stated the following -

"What is government itself but the greatest of all reflections on human nature? If men were angels, no government would be necessary..."

Americans have been tricked into believing that they are unable to provide for themselves without major government intervention. Many people expect government to help "guide" them in the right direction. Have we become incapable of self-governing? Should we let government do for us instead of doing for ourselves? I must remind you that this frame of mind is not what helped make America and Americans the greatest nation and the most civilized nation that has ever walked this Earth. It was our independent, pioneering spirit that led to a huge leap forward.

America's founders revolutionized government with the introduction of the concept known as "self government". This gave birth to the industrial and technological revolutions that propelled the world into something that most generations could never have dreamed up.

The spirit of exploration and achievement is still inside each of us today. It does not matter if you are a taxpayer or tax consumer, greatness can be achieved through dedication and hard work. Americans need to step out of the government's shadow and shed our dependent mentality. The American Taxslaves can flourish once again. We can only achieve this if we free ourselves from an abusive political ruling class. Awaken your revolutionary spirit and do what you are capable of doing - you will surprise yourself. We will shake things up for the better. We must force ourselves to be independent, accountable and responsible for our own decisions and actions.

Government has no business intruding in our lives, homes, economy and our workplace. **Government influence has perverted a once free and**

independent country of explorers and creators. It is our responsibility as a free society to dismantle the current tax and spend system of government greed. It is time to regulate government spending on all levels. Local, state and federal spending must be restrained. Taxes must be cut across the board. Taxpayers have managed to do more with less, now it is time for our rulers in government to do the same.

This will be a tough lesson to teach, and there will be great opposition but is necessary if we hope to break free from the bondage of economic enslavement that holds us captive. **We can and must get the enemy called Big Government under control - we have learned the hard way that it cannot control itself.**

Our current government is a façade with puppets in the front positions. Special interests and big vote buying public employee unions now pull the strings. **Americans have been sold the generic alternative to government - we need the real thing.** Social programs and huge government pensions have made Taxslaves of the American taxpayers. We must regain political power by fighting against our rulers with courage. The time has come for us to launch a rational and emotional attack on the enemies of liberty and independence. The American Taxslaves cannot afford to take part in the vote buying game for another election cycle. If we do, we will remain Tax Peasants and subjects to our rulers. Instead, we need to focus on principles and actions - not just words and nonstop contradictions. It is impossible to buy more and cut spending. Taxpayers cannot get away with this in their homes, so how can government do it? Borrowing more and taxing more is not an option.

My freedom is not up for sale or for rent, and this is not up for negotiation.

Most Americans from my generation (age thirty or so) are unable to wrap their minds around the thought of a world without government handouts and the warm embrace of social dependence policies.

We have become victims of our own self-imposed stupidity.

Marxism has been brilliantly marketed to us inside the appealing package of "compassion" —and we bought right into it. The principles of personal responsibility and limited government have no place in a society of unconcerned, materialistic sheep-citizens. It is time for a firm reminder that each program created by government is paid for by the taxpayers. Each tax increase represents a reduction in our liberty. The economic burden imposed on taxpayers by government has within it the seeds of destruction. This applies to businesses as well, not the Exxon Mobil, Microsoft, AIG, or other huge industry monsters of the world, but the small business owners trying to get a great idea or product off the ground. It is now time to support the hungry entrepreneur who wants to make his own way - without answering to levels of corporate management. Unfortunately, these independent minded, motivated and talented American entrepreneurs are suffering from serious tax burdens that are imposed by useless layers of government and reckless legislation. Taxes act as a barrier to American prosperity. Small business failures are incorrectly labeled "market failures", when in reality they are government imposed failures. The rulers in government have forcibly perverted the economic system for small businesses by sabotaging the entrepreneurial spirit.

Elected and appointed officials are confiscating the income of hard working taxpayers who already sacrifice enough in order to manage and sustain their own lives. Instead of encouraging the entrepreneurs, our political ruling class will do anything to hold on to their power - even if it means destroying the spirit of American innovation. Their target is our income and we must protect the result of our labor. Our earnings represent our work and our achievements. The right to keep our earnings is essentially the basis for our freedom.

"Vote buying" has become common in our heavily corrupted, politically correct time. Any American that stands in opposition to social programs or unrealistic government spending is unfairly labeled a "racist" or a "bigot". Taxpayers must fight tirelessly against this false "marketing" onslaught that has been encouraged by our ruling class. **We must hold our ground long enough for the majority of Americans to wake up from a politically induced coma.** Taxpayers are the generals standing on the front line fighting for economic independence. It is up to the taxpaying portion of society to defend their financial freedom. American Taxslaves must to longer accept the current political scheme that strips us of our time, effort, hard work and earned income.

Our political salvation will be realized when we say no to Big Government and yes to personal accountability. The choice is ours to make. I have made up my mind. Millions of Americans have yet to wake up and take back what is theirs - political and economic freedom from the oppressive masters of our political ruling class. We must elect officials who are willing to introduce legislation designed to forcibly remove the perversion of our economic freedom. We have tools of opportunity at our disposal that we can use to correct the corruption of our freedoms. We must expand our influence as taxpaying Americans who want to rightfully keep what we earn. Our work ethic is a reflection of our lives, our independence, and our economic freedom to succeed and embrace the American Dream. Freedom is not a right of passage; it is something that must be jealously guarded. American Taxslaves must wake up from the economic nightmare that has been forced upon us. We can all become hard-working men and women - because at heart we are more alike than we are different. Unfortunately, some of us just drank too much of the government supplied Cool-Aid. Enlightened taxpayers must pump the stomachs of their sleeping neighbors. It is our responsibility to remove the poison of dependence on Big Government from their blood streams.

American taxpayers should take an honest look at who is responsible for the problems we currently face. Look no further than your front door. The problem is you, your family, your friends and your neighbors. These are the true culprits - the people too uninvolved and un-concerned to embrace and work for real change. The majority of Americans have become politically lazy and accepting of the political "spell" of our ruling class. Americans who are unconcerned, uninvolved, and unaware are the true barriers to progress, economic prosperity and true freedom.

The British statesman Edmund Burke said the following:

"The only thing necessary for the triumph of evil is for good men to do nothing".

Most people make no attempt to serve their own best interests when it comes to politics and economic independence. We can work a 50 hour work week, but just ask a neighbor the last time they voted on their local school budget and you will see them turn into a deer staring into headlights. Most Americans don't know better because they are not equipped with the tools required to take back control of our government. Most people refuse to put in the effort that it takes to live like free men. It is up to you, the enlightened, involved American Taxslave to take them by the hand and lead them to a better place - where hard working men and women keep more of what they earn. Those who live in the darkness of "political ignorance" are the barriers standing in our way.

We must infuse our neighbors and our communities with common sense and political enlightenment. Energize them with a combination of passion and knowledge. Do not demand their participation; instead appeal to their self-interests. We all want the same thing – we want to keep what we earn and with it, create better and more economically stable lives for our families.

Is anyone else extremely concerned that the lunatics are now running the asylum? I cannot figure out who is crazier, the elected officials - the Tax Terrorists in public office - or the people that continually re-elect them. We cannot continue to allow their lack of concern to damage our lives beyond repair. Because of our inattentiveness we have given our ruling class a free pass to steal the income of hard working, taxpaying Americans. The burden we are asked to bear for government programs is beyond the brink of intolerable. In his Socialist integration manual- a book titled *Rules for Radicals* (a favorite of Obama and Hillary) Sol Alinsky, outlined his "ends justify the means" reasoning. Taxpayers must apply this same thinking in our quest to restore accountability and resurrect the time-tested principles of liberty, independence and self-reliance.

I refuse to embrace the enslaving nature of the radically progressive - tax and spend idea of Big Government politicians. They have already planted the seeds of economic failure. It is time for us to dig the seeds up and rip them from the soil before the roots grab hold. Our ruling class has implemented the formula for failure. Now, we must implement the solution for success. Americans must respond to the attacks on our freedom with strength in numbers. Taxpayer unity and loyalty is in our mutual self interests. We must adhere to the principles of freedom, personal accountability and a resolute commitment to restore limited government. This is a quest to restore sanity in our government. Remember this; **Slaves give in, warriors fight back.** The basic laws of economics show us that if we spend more than we earn we will operate at a financial loss. The consequences are predictable if we simply look at the facts. That is what keeps taxpaying homeowner's budget conscious. Unfortunately for taxpayers and homeowners, the various levels of government are unable to see the consequences of uncontrolled spending. We must force our elected leaders to apply common sense to their spending habits. If government does not have enough money coming from a revenue base to spend on a new program, then they must not spend it. They must not spend it now or commit to spending it at a later date. Taxpayers are forced to pay for the expensive political promises of our ruling class.

What is my joy if all hands, even the unclean, can reach into it?

What is my wisdom, if even the fools can dictate to me?

What is my freedom, if all creatures, even the botched and the impotent are my masters?

What is my life, if I am but to bow, to agree and to obey?

But I am done with this creed of corruption.

I am done with the monster of "We", the word of serfdom, of plunder, of misery falsehood and shame.

-**Ayn Rand**

The Rules of Political Warfare: There Are No Rules

I am sick and tired of feeling like an ATM - an **Abused Taxpaying Machine.** It is time to put an "OUT OF ORDER: EMPTY" sign around our necks. We are not here to fund Big Government and its wasteful programs. Responsible, taxpaying Americans have learned slowly but surely that government officials are unconstrained when it comes to spending and cowardly when it comes to making tough financial decisions. Spending what American taxpayers do not have is a reckless decision.

Americans are currently living under the rule of ruthless Tax Junkies who will do anything for their next fix. We must force them to admit that they have a problem and conduct a Tax-aholics anonymous meeting at the voting booths. Failure at the voting booths will be a very sobering experience for them. Politics has become show business and politicians are now the showmen. Because of this transformation, we are unable to make accurate sense of what is really going on in the political world around us. Truth is mixed with lies, leaving the American taxpayers to fend for themselves and filter through the wreckage of political antagonism. We have no solid information to use as a guide to make decisions for our own economic survival. Political sharks create their own context and importance by claiming to be just like you and I. Sure; they want us to believe they are just average taxpayers and "good old Joe the Plumber" types. The reality is that they earn a living at our expense. One great example of this is Federal Government grants for liberal districts, which in return provide favorable votes on specific legislation like "free" healthcare. Lies have replaced the truth. We are living in an unrealistic, imaginary and fabricated world. It is up to the entire voting block of taxpayers to make "change" real. **"Care giving" must not be the responsibility of our government.**

In her speech at the 2008 Democratic national Convention, Michelle Obama stated *"We committed ourselves to building the world as it should be"*. I think all of us know how much the Obama administration has spent in the first year since that statement was made. I do not recall reading in our Constitution that it is the president or any branch of government's responsibility to "build the world as it should be".

The primary purpose of the government is to protect our freedom. Didn't you know? The proper role of the government is to ensure the liberty and freedom of the people. It is not the responsibility of our government to stimulate the economy, create jobs or "legally" confiscate our earnings only to redistribute it as they see fit. Where did we go wrong? Taxpayers should be outraged at the above statement. Taxpayers are the people who will write the checks that will be used to "build the world as it should be". All of the American taxpayers combined cannot write a check that big.

There is huge potential for danger when money is in the wrong hands (political contributions). Public relations firms advertise and create a fabricated image of politicians that seek office. Back in 1959 a TV Guide article quoted John F. Kennedy when he stated the following:

"Television is a medium that lends itself to manipulation, exploitation and gimmicks. Political campaigns can actually be taken over by public relations experts who tell the candidate how to use TV, what to say, what to stand for and what kind of person to be".

This statement is very scary, due to the simple fact that it is true; this has become a sad reality. Kennedy's statement represents the very thing that our republic was never intended to be - a popularity contest, administered by a powerful political ruling class. Big Government is a one-way street with a no U-turn sign at every intersection. Taxation is conflict oriented, not common sense oriented. Too few elected officials are willing to encourage conversation regarding the issues that we are faced with. Taxpayers are the ultimate financiers of our society. As an American, a taxpayer and a homeowner, I believe we are on a terrible path to economic destruction. Americans are demanding that government "create" jobs when in fact it is not the role of government to do so. In difficult economic times job creation becomes the single greatest campaign promise politicians make.

We must ask ourselves; at what cost? This is my country and my home. So I will fight alone if I have to. I am ready to show these greedy, unworthy men to the door politely or throw them out peacefully but forcefully. Our constitution has been taken for granted for too long. "We the People" make up the best part of this country – not those serving in government. What does this tell us about ourselves? It tells us that we are not as free and independent as we think we are. In regard to our political process, Americans are no longer brave; we have become cowardly dependents on Big Government. It's almost like we are little children who do not want to make our abusive mommy and daddy angry; so we deal with it. You cannot appease a bully; they will only grow more aggressive and threatening.

Taxpayers are like scared little children who sit quietly in the corner; terrified to make a peep. We are afraid of our government because of what they can take away from us. Because of this, we have essentially handed over our individual liberties for the sake of keeping our nice homes, fancy cars, and new designer shoes in a desperate attempt to satisfy our uncontrolled appetite for material things. I am no exception to this; I am guilty of it as well. It is time to hit the emergency brakes. The spending in Washington, as well as in local layers of government, is killing taxpayers. Essentially, the power hungry politicians have built a wall between the taxpayers and the tax consumers. Although the animosity is stirring, we are smart enough to place blame where it belongs - on the vote seeking, service promising, power hungry Tax Terrorist politicians. **All Americans- taxpayers and tax consumers alike have been endowed with the blessings that freedom has provided for us.** Looking to the government for handouts or employment is not the answer. Rather, look inward at yourself, to your own inner strength. Achievement is created from necessity. When we are facing our biggest challenges we have a choice - fight or give up. Those of us who have worked our way through our greatest obstacles have learned how strong we really are. Our will to survive and beat the overwhelming odds only comes out when we are forced to fight our way out of a scary situation. *Life is a series of peaks and valleys. It is what you do when you are alone in the valley that determines who you are.* In other words, when you are on a peak or a high point, life is good. When you are in the valley - the low point - life is hard. It is at your lowest point where you truly realize the strength of your character. Will you climb out by being resourceful? Or will you give in and submit to the odds that are stacked against you. The things that you do when you are in the deepest part of the valley, with no clear way out, will determine who you are. I know who I am; I will crawl my way out until my fingertips are bloodied to the bone before I give up. Come hell or high water, you can bet I am getting out of any situation that is within my power to escape!

In the words of the great American revolutionary Patrick Henry and the Mexican revolutionary Emiliano Zapata Salazar:

"Give me liberty or give me death"...because "I would rather die on my feet than live on my knees".

Life without challenges is not worth living because you never truly get to know if you are capable of being a leader. History has proven that in times of great conflict true leaders always appear. These are the leaders who will ascend to the top and become motivators of men. We cannot always control our circumstances, but we can control ourselves despite the circumstances. If you want to lead, take charge and don't look back.

American citizens must begin to sort the truth from the lies. This will not only help us, but it will help preserve America for generations to come. We must pass on the torch of liberty and freedom that has blessed and enriched our lives. We cannot forget that our founding fathers fought and sacrificed their lives in an attempt to escape the oppressive British government. It is now time for us to say, "Enough is enough". We are not done fighting for freedom 234 years later. The idea of true freedom has become foreign to many modern day Americans. **We must once again become revolutionaries who fight for the survival of our Republic.** As an American, it is your duty to go out and unite with your neighbors. That is what it will take to cross the finish line of victory. We must have an uprising of like-minded, independent Americans who seek freedom and live their lives in anticipation of achieving this goal. America must transform itself back into a united, indivisible nation of people that appreciate the opportunity to earn a living in hope of a better life. We can no longer allow ourselves to be a nation of takers; cowardly tax peasants who are too timid and afraid to earn our own way without government ensuring our existence. American citizens must resist the temptation to allow government to take care of their needs. This kind of behavior is not reflective of what American represents - it is not freedom or independence...it is slavery. America's founding fathers were radicals simply because they wanted to be left alone. They wanted to be responsible for their own success or their own failure. We have recently become a society that is obsessed with radicals; just look at all the Americans who are wearing Che Guerva tee shirts. We must learn about our enemies and study the details of how the Communist, Marxist and Socialist movements came to power throughout history. Read about the progressive agendas of Woodrow Wilson, Roosevelt's "New Deal" and Lyndon B. Johnson's "Great Society". Look at the last century of legislation and see for yourself how Socialism seduced the American people. Socialism has indeed arrived. You should be curious as to how it weaseled its way into our shores. When will we wake up? Will it be when the spell of our ruling class wears off? My answer is No! We will snap out if it when we are fed up with acting like servants to a lawless political ruling class that deceives and divides the people of these United American States.

Most American taxpayers do nothing to curb the government's appetite for tax dollars. As a result, we are part of the problem. We must now become the solution. Failure to take action will only seal our fate and make things worse. When will the tax madness end? Who will hold these irresponsible officials responsible for their reckless actions? The responsibility can only fall on the shoulders of the American Taxslaves. **Combative political action must be taken immediately.**

America is badly in need of small government - made up of men and women who believe in personal responsibility and will work towards a restoration of personal accountability. **The problem is not Democrats. The problem is not Republicans. The problem is both.** However, the biggest problem is us-the indifferent, uninvolved, unconcerned American taxpayers. Citizens must hold all elected officials in both political parties to their Constitutional duties. Our problem goes beyond party loyalty. We must elect people to office that will stand up for the right values and do what is right and necessary, a restoration of our Constitutionally limited Republic. Our current "leaders" have no sense of what is going on in our homes. **The truth is, we are being terrorized by abusive taxation.** Governments collect the checks; we the taxpayers write those checks. Reform is our responsibility, so it is our battle to fight. I have an urgent message for taxpayers. The phone number is the same; the Constitution is still on the other end of the line. All we have to do is dial the number.

While taxpayers are breaking their backs, taxation is breaking our hearts. As Americans, it is our responsibility to be the adhesive that bonds politicians to their duties. We are no longer living the American Dream. Instead, we are living the American Nightmare. Laziness, entitlement, government handouts to dependant voting blocks and public employee unions have all devastated our great nation and the individual freedom it once represented. **As Taxslaves, we must force ourselves out of political exile and become stronger, smarter and more involved than we have been.** We need to take a good look at the cost of Big Government and figure out how to reduce it down to size.

The political betrayal of our rulers is evident. An American Awakening is coming. **Conservatism is no longer in exile.**

Taxpayers have been reduced to Taxslaves. Now we must begin to take steps to preserve our own self-interests.

The days of Big Government are coming to an end. It is time for taxpayers to take drastic measures so that we can fix the problem of a clever, swindling ruling class. We must elect people that are ready to balance the budget and operate on a surplus - not a deficit. Our current elected officials are unwilling to make the necessary cuts that will free the Taxslaves of America. We cannot operate only to avoid bankruptcy; we should work with an underlying desire to prosper economically. There is no way we can spend our way out of this fiscal mess. More government spending only leads to higher taxes. **Taxation is the fruit from a poisonous tree called dependence.**

What do we have to lose by not taking action? Our freedom is now at stake. What do you plan to do about it? Government knows that "We the People" have become political cowards. Taxpayers have become political cowards. The majority of us have become afraid of our own government. For the first time in our history, Americans are too hopeless to speak out on behalf of what is right. Politicians in Washington and those in your city hall do not care about you. Their only concern is how much they can get from you. Most members of our political ruling class lack honor and character. Politicians simply seize power and rule with an iron fist. They scare us into spending. We are left hoping that our taxes do not go up too much, so we are passive, obedient and accepting of their reckless ways - like good little Taxslaves. American taxpayers have demanded that the rulers cut the spending, but they do not listen to us. Instead, our lawless political ruling class continues to govern in opposition to the will of the people. The spiral into economic enslavement has been forced upon us. How can we trust men and women who take and take but do not provide for those they have taken from? **Prosperity in America will end if this behavior continues.** Our country, our lives, and our freedom as we know it will disappear if we continue to sit by and do nothing. We cannot allow the reckless behavior of our career politicians to continue happening at such a rapid rate. Get on the phone and call your senators, congressmen and local representatives. Demand that they stop the spending. See what happens – they will simply ignore you. That is why it is important to make sure that your elected officials never get on a ballot again if they do not stand on the side of the taxpayers. If our elected "leaders" do not serve the best interests of taxpayers, you better stand at the voting booths with a small army of local taxpayers ready to give them the boot. Dedicate all of your free time and available resources to remove these men and women from office. We must make it clear to them that if they want to "serve" then that is exactly what they must do – serve, not rule. If politicians do not serve within the restrictions laid out by the voting taxpayers they must bow out gracefully or be removed.

Our current elected officials have damned themselves by their lack of support for the taxpaying portion of our country. In addition, it is appropriate to mention that their actions are unconstitutional. **Slick talking politicians, special interest groups and other tax consumers are intellectually and economically raping the taxpayers.** The current rate of government spending is unsustainable. The pocket pillaging must come to an end. Taxpayers can no longer be used as fuel for the political system. America is going broke as a nation. Hard working taxpayers will be left with nothing if the current tax madness continues to go unchallenged. If this keeps up, everything we have earned as a nation will be lost.

We must embrace personal responsibility and set an example for those who are hopeless. Become a contagious flame. Let us burn down the house of dependence. America was built on the idea of personal responsibility – so be accountable for yourself and stand on your own.

America is strong because the people are the foundation. This is a call to action to all hard working American Taxslaves; it is your responsibility to do the right thing and lead the way. Borrow from the blueprint of American history and go beyond the restrictions forced on us by the present day Tax Tyrants?

I am ready to stand and fight. I hope you are too.

We are treated to the "positive" news reports daily; millions of taxpaying Americans are facing financial ruin. Each of us must work hard to stabilize our economic lives. This can only be achieved through freedom and independence from a treacherous, tax crazed government. The current tax and spend frenzy cannot last forever. All trends must come to an end, and our current financial meltdown is no exception.

We are facing an economic crisis - it has evolved from a leadership crisis. It is a result of blatant failures on the part of our elected leaders who have been unable to produce balanced budgets and say no to spending money that we cannot afford to spend. In the course of our daily lives we purchase many different products and services. In all cases, we try to get the most we can for our money. When we elect a politician we are making a financial decision - perhaps one of the most critical decisions that will directly contribute to our financial happiness or our financial misery. Just like buying a new car, home, or sweater, we must select our elected officials based on factors like cost, quality, durability, reliability and strength. If you are a taxpayer like I am, you probably feel as if you have not got your moneys worth in a long time.

Politicians on all levels of government must be held responsible for their actions. This is especially true locally where taxpayers have the most direct influence. Do your research before casting your vote. Has the candidate voted in favor of tax increases? Are the budgets growing bigger and bigger year after year? If so, why? What was in it for you the taxpayer? Look back and ask the question "Was the tax increase worth it"? **Only by keeping the Tax Terrorists on a short leash will we be able to control them and therefore keep ourselves off the brink of financial disaster for another day.**

Have you ever found a great parking spot, only to realize that you do not have a quarter in your pocket to "feed the meter"? If so, I am sure you pulled into the vacant spot and desperately searched your car seats for change? You suddenly feel a sense of relief and joy when you find the quarter that will allow you to avoid a parking ticket and go about your intended business. You proceed to insert the quarter and "feed the meter" only to find the machine "eats it". The quarter disappears and the time does not register on the parking meter. Have you ever experienced this? What do you feel at this moment? Try to re-capture the feeling for a moment. It is painfully frustrating - you feel let down. You did what was asked of you with a certain expectation- "feed the meter" and go about your business. But no, instead the meter ripped you off and now if you carry on with your business a meter maid will ticket you. So now, frustrated and disappointed, you are forced to leave your convenient parking spot. Due to the failure of a system outside of your control, you must now make other arrangements. Soon we will have to give up more than our parking spots. In time we will be forced to give up our homes, our future, our freedom and ourselves to a system of government that does not work - because it is letting us down like a broken parking meter.

In 2009, amidst the national healthcare debate, reverend Jesse Jackson vocalized his shock and outrage that black men and women were opposed to the proposed national healthcare program. When did it become a requirement for black Americans to support huge Socialist government programs? That type of thinking (especially coming from a civil rights activist) is blatantly racist. This is an example of divisive politics and a clear attempt to draw a racial divide. Maybe it has not occurred to Rev. Jackson that there are millions of black men and women who are true patriots that love their American freedoms and do not want to be ruled by Big Government.

Many White, Black, Latin, Mexican, Asian, Blue, Black, Pink, Red, Green, Orange, Yellow, Purple and many other people of different nationalities and colors believe in limited government and indeed want to keep what they earn. **Most taxpayers, regardless of physical differences do not want to constantly feed their income to the tax consuming part of society.** Americans from all backgrounds still believe in small, non-intrusive government and personal responsibility. Our "leaders" have it wrong – **Big Government is not the answer.** As a nation of taxpayers, we have the ability to thrive. Even though many Americans fail to realize it, we still have the courage to fight back against Big Government and abusive spending. The greatest loss in all of this tax madness is the potential that is wasted. Unrealized potential is the greatest of all things wasted. American taxpayers must have a firm understanding of the damage done by unbridled government spending. American Taxslaves know what is needed and what is wasteful. The facts must be laid out, as they exist, without economic slant or political rhetoric. Most Americans refuse to see the truth because it has become tangled in so many lies. America's greatest loss has been the hope for a better future. It is time to regain our courage and live free from government perversion of the free market system of development and trade – lower taxes don't hurt either.

It is time for a Taxpayers Emancipation Proclamation

Taxpayers have lost their way. The "leaders" who we trusted have deliberately misled us. They have taken us down the path to Tax Slavery.

It is time to free the American Tax Slaves.

For the past 100 years we have come to accept progressives in Big Government. Why have we accepted their tax and spend abuse of working men and women. Their rise to power does not make sense to me. It would make a good novel, but not a good life for taxpayers. Even novels must make sense. We currently believe that we are "free" despite the fact that our government takes more than half of what we earn. Our acceptance of this does not make sense. Most taxpayers are respectable people. We do what is asked of us. Most of us do it while kicking, screaming and complaining - but nonetheless we do what is asked of us. The question now has become; how much more can government ask of us? When you are "asked" to do something you can say "No". Try saying "No" to the IRS. So, now the answer to the question of "how much more can they take from us" will be answered by our actions and the resistance we show in the face of their irrational economic demands. Make no mistake about it - our political ruling class is forcibly taking our hard earned income. They confiscate our earnings, steal from our families and severely limit the quality of our lives in the process. Even if you do not have a family and just simply choose to spend your earnings on lavish or unnecessary things, your income is the product of your effort - so go spend it as you choose to. Your earnings are yours to do what you want with. Control of your earnings represents your economic freedom. **It is your right, and your economic sovereignty to do as you wish with what you put in the time and effort to earn.**

Ask yourself the following question:

"Is government working tirelessly on my behalf"?

Are elected officials doing everything they can do to support the best interests of taxpayers and property owners? The simple answer is no. They are not looking out for our freedom, our pockets or our ability to live our lives without over-reaching government interference. Most of us are not financially secure or comfortable. Most American taxpayers are struggling - barely hanging on to what they earn. The American Taxslaves are hanging on by a thread just to get by from paycheck to paycheck. We have an undeniable right as free men and women to keep the majority of our earned income. We should not only keep 30% to 50% of our earnings, but instead a more favorable 85% to 90%. Do you honestly believe that our "leaders" are committed to helping us do this? I cannot see it happening without a massive uprising of the American Taxslaves.

What if I told you a "fictitious" story about a country made up of hard working people that have been economically enslaved by government taxation. What if I laid out details that match our own situation, then told you it took place in some foreign land? Chances are you would believe the story if it related to another country. But, most people would never believe that this story actually takes place in America. People would cry out "not in our beloved country - after all, we are free". Unfortunately, we must face the sad fact that the story is not fictitious and it does not take place in some far off land. It is happening now - right here in America. If taxpaying Americans actually read a list of all the taxes that they are forced to pay - both directly and indirectly – Americans would be in an uproar of politically induced rage. Most Americans would never believe that an economic assault like this could happen in the "Land of the free and the home of the brave". Hard working Americans may no longer be free, but the American Taxslaves are brave. We get up everyday and go to work, so that we can pay our taxes and our bills. We may not always do it with a smile on our face but we still get it done. As taxpayers, we must exonerate ourselves from the charges of taxation levied against us from an oppressive government. It is time to launch a Taxpayer Militia.

Many people fight for "fairness" by providing support for social programs that help people in need. This is a pro-tax consumer and anti-tax payer system. Where is the justice in being taxed out of our homes? Is justice served when the earnings of working class people is confiscated by government and re-distributed to a part of society that may not have sacrificed to create the same opportunities that the so called "prosperous" segment has created for themselves? It is no secret that some people are just plain lazy and take advantage of the "system". Where is the fairness and justice when it comes to taking care of taxpayers? Where is the acknowledgement of our struggle?

The overwhelming majorities of working class Americans are not wealthy. Most Americans are not even on secure financial ground. **Economic and social engineering must come to a quick and immediate end.**

Karl Marx said, *"From each according to his ability, to each according to his need".*

I believe, *"To each the result of what he works for and achieves on his own merit".*

In other words, I believe that each American should keep what they go out and earn - despite the inability of another person to work for his or her own needs. Another way to put it is - if you can work, but choose not to, you will not get it from government. The reason why? Government gets money from taxpayers and redistributes it to tax consumers. What will our future be like if we continue to support the capable, but lazy, unmotivated portion of society? I refuse to continually give what I work for and earn to those that do not work and earn it.

There is a tax harvest going on and the Taxslaves are the crops that produce. We are producing more tax dollars at a rapid rate for the Tax Farmers of government.

It amazes me that people can find a way to get themselves up at 3 O'clock in the morning on "Black Friday" (The day after Thanksgiving - the biggest shopping day of the year) to camp out on long lines in order to save a few bucks and shop for things that they do not really need. I will confidently bet that those same people would not exert one fraction of that same effort to camp out on the lawn of their local city hall, state government building or outside of their federal district representative's home before a vote on a proposed tax increase. If the same "bargain hunters" put just a fraction of the effort expended on "Black Friday" shopping into an effort to hold politicians accountable and reduce taxes we would be much better off as a country. America has a problem because most people are willing to put in the effort to save a few bucks shopping, but they are unable to contribute that same effort with fierce tenacity and dedication towards reform of government spending. Taxpayers have the most to lose. Because of this, we must work hard to put the right people in office. We must find - and elect people that are dedicated to cutting budgets and committed to radically slash spending. If we can cut wasteful spending programs, taxpayers will be able to save a great deal more money than ever could on "Black Friday".

We need to work on dropping the price of government.

There is income inequality in America – there always has been and there always will be. This is because there is effort inequality. People make less because they do less and aspire for less. This is not true in every case, but it is in most cases. **Most income inequality is a direct result of effort inequality.** Some of us are just "effortly" challenged. Taxpayers are constantly under assault by politicians and special interest groups who devise schemes to find new ways to legally confiscate our earned income. They in effect "rob" us of our time and effort. The American Taxslaves work and sacrifice for what they earn. Yes indeed there is inequality and it is a direct result of government taking from the taxpaying portion of society and giving it to the tax consuming part of society. It is wrong to take from a person that earns his or her own living and gives it to another person that has not earned it. As individuals, it is our responsibility to reduce dependence levels. Unsustainable debt and risky financial decisions have contributed to our economic troubles. We cause our own problems by borrowing too much and spending too much

There are fewer obstacles placed in our way by other people than those that we place upon ourselves. Our limitations are self-imposed. We must teach future generations to understand that not everyone is going to be a millionaire. Can it happen? Yes but most of us do not give ourselves enough credit to make the effort to do what it takes to become successful. Success can be defined in many different ways. It is based on our individual idea of success. Financial success means having a lot of money - because that allows us to have security and economic independence. Most of us do not take the time or make the effort to do the things that will bring potential success. It is our responsibility as individuals to create the right conditions for success to happen. Although it very well may not happen, we must put ourselves in a position to succeed so that when an opportunity comes along we can jump on it and make an attempt to do something that will allow prosperity. Success is not guaranteed, but we must put in the effort if we hope to have a chance. Entrepreneurs are dissuaded by excessive taxation, licensing, red tape, bureaucracy and other government imposed obstacles. All we need to do is look at the tax code- (as of 2006) 60, 000 + pages of bureaucratic filth. This is a huge deviation from the original 400 pages in 1913 upon its inception. Government acts as a hostile deterrent to entrepreneurial achievement. The amount of tax that businesses are forced pay does not allow small startups to save enough capital (money), fast enough to invest in good short-term business growth opportunities. Instead, startup businesses and individuals are forced to take out loans and be weighed down by interest payments, payroll taxes and other obstacles that are placed in the way by government and banks.

Income equality is not a reasonable goal unless wealth re-distribution is administered. This form of "legal" extortion degenerates our workforce and ambition of American workers. There will always be portions of society that are bottom feeders. These are people that do as little as possible but still expect equal pay for their time and only give minimum effort. Bottom feeders come in all colors, shapes and sizes. They do not deserve more simply because they are at the bottom of the economic totem pole. I made a decision, just as many other Americans have - to provide for myself. I have created the conditions for my own success. I achieved my short-term goals by doing more and producing more than I am paid to do. I constantly educate myself through reading, learning and embracing new experiences. **Responsibility scares the heck out of me – but I have no other choice – it's sink or swim. I know that if I challenge myself, I will get better with each passing challenge.** Some people get fired from a job and then have the audacity to demand that government pay them unemployment. These "career" dependents must be forced to get up off their behinds and find a job that will provide a source of income. They must learn to live off something other than a government handout. Nothing is "free". Ultimately the "government" funding always comes out of the pockets of American taxpayers. Now is a good time to remind you of the old saying "Money doesn't grow on trees" - it comes from working men and women who earn a living and pay their taxes. I have some advice for the "career dependants" - get a job and work your way up. If you have to, start by flipping burgers. Take on a second job to supplement your income - perhaps a night shift somewhere else. Do this to bridge the gap between work opportunities. If you learn to provide for your own needs through sacrifice and hard work, achievement will become the cornerstone of your life.

It is not the responsibility of government - on any level-to take care of its' citizen's finances by taking from one to give to another.

Achievement and prosperity come from sacrifice, hard work and the individual will to survive. Leave the "charitable" work to the people in our communities - not government. Remember, government has no wealth or money of its own, only what it forcibly confiscates from the working class of taxpayers. Government owes its existence to the taxpayers because our "funding" keeps it operable.

It is time to starve the beast of Big Government.

Government on any level cannot operate without taxpayer dollars as fuel. The problem is that taxpayers are shoved to the side like second-class citizens. We are "forced" to fund Big Government programs that make unrealistic promises - no matter how detrimental it is to our personal lives.

The main function of government, as our founding fathers intended, is to make sure that one person does not harm another and to help citizens in the event of a disaster that local communities are not equipped to handle. **Our government was not created to take the earnings of one citizen and redistribute it to another - just to make things fair.** Most of us wonder when this Tax Oppression will end. When will the abusive, excessive social re-engineering through wealth distribution come to an end? The answer is simple, when "We the Taxslaves" put an end to it! Taxpayers must campaign and vote for real change. The tax madness will end when the vested taxpayers encourage honest people to run for office. America needs leaders who are committed to slashing budgets and willing to cut spending by up to Ninety percent. Taxpaying Americans need to clean house on Election Day. The answer to the question of "When will this madness come to an end?" is simple. It will end when the American Taxslaves decide to end this tax madness.

Americans are not born talented; they spend a lifetime working to develop their knowledge and skills. Because of this fact, each of us is entitled to keep the product of our labor. Excessive taxation prevents working people from keeping the result of their work. Americans do not suddenly wake up one day economically safe and secure (unless they hit the lottery). The overwhelming majority of successful business owners (entrepreneurs) and taxpayers achieve prosperity through hard work and sacrifice. They produce wealth (I do not necessarily mean rich) only to have it confiscated by government to be re distributed to those at the bottom of the tax totem pole - those who have not climbed their way up off of the government "payroll" into the free market. Instead of climbing, they are encouraged by ruthless politicians to go out and vote for the people that promise to take from the taxpayers and give to the tax consumers. This involves long-term social welfare recipients, politicians, public employee unions, special interest groups and the biggest culprit; government employees. Too many Americans have failed to realize their full potential. This is due to our dependent frame of mind. Once someone says, "Hard work pays off", suddenly it's a whole different story. You hear things like – "I do not get paid enough to work those hours," "That's not my job," or the best excuse is "Why work when I can make the same amount of money on unemployment". As free individuals, we must put in the time and energy to make ourselves better - there can be no excuses. Currently, working class taxpayers are being punished for being "successful". It is tough to call middle class Americans like myself "successful" in the financial sense, but that is what is happening to our country. The American Dream of homeownership suddenly makes us "rich" in the eyes of others that have not sacrificed as much as we did.

Our progressive Federal Income Tax punishes success. **Our political ruling class punishes achievement and rewards laziness in return for votes.** Most middle class "successful" taxpayers had to take out loans to put themselves through college, graduate, medical or trade schools to get where they are now. In most cases it was not handed to them. Instead, they earned it the good old-fashioned way. Tax consumers and government employees are awarded grants and tuition assistance "gifts" based on racial and economic conditions. Tax consumers get to go to school for free because the taxpaying portion of society is forced to pay for it. Although many succeed and gain an opportunity that they would not otherwise have achieved. Regardless of this, we must all earn our own way. The beauty of freedom is this - we all have the freedom to try, the freedom to fail, and the freedom to succeed. In other words, we have true liberty – but it is fading fast. It is time for the American Taxslaves to put on their work boots and pull themselves out of economic enslavement. It is time to get to work. **We must not allow our "leaders" to re-distribute our earnings as they see fit based on the amount of votes it will produce for them.** Re-election can no longer be the primary focus of those in office, that is the easy route.

We must force our elected officials to start doing what is right, not what is easy – force them to start governing efficiently.

All levels of government could use a good house cleaning. Officials must begin to operate leaner, faster and more efficiently. Is there a single taxpayer that seriously believes the current government is loyally serving the people?

It breaks my heart to see so many Americans with nothing to say about the criminal behavior of our government officials. American taxpayers put such little effort into themselves on a political level. **A huge disconnect exists between government and the taxpaying public.** There is a severe conflict of interests between the political ruling class and the people. Elected officials are not doing what they were put in office to do. They refuse to effectively serve the public. Politicians "work" to "create" more jobs, more complex legislation and as a result more complex problems. They devise plots to make American taxpayers part with their hard earned income (economic property). The days of Big Government must come to an end. The time of individual responsibility and personal leadership must arrive. In the wake of Big Government, taxpayers will be freed from the economic enslavement caused by excessive taxation. Only then can we truly live free. We will be responsible for taking care of our own needs. It is a lofty task, but I am up for the challenge. Are you?

Government will not care about you more than you care about yourself. It is time for both taxpayers and tax consumers to start taking care of their own needs. Stop waiting for the government to do it for you. **The words "Of the people, by the people and for the people" need to ring in the ears of elected officials throughout this country.** Thoughts of freedom must be prevalent, constantly present 24 hours a day in our minds. Eat, sleep, and breathe personal responsibility - not dependence on Big Government. Taxpayers are becoming irritated, resentful and desperate. "We the People" are fed up with the blatant disregard that our government officials show for the hard work that we do on a daily basis. We are fighting just to survive economically. The American Taxslaves are enraged at the reckless government spending that has forced us into indentured servitude. Our rulers display arrogance through their use of government policies and wasteful social programs. Needless waste and reckless dishonesty has become a common operating practice in government. This is the reason why we have seen such an outcry from TEA Party activists.

The American Taxslaves must wage a war against the political class. We must cause political chaos. **Legislative power is the only real means to attaining our goal of a responsive and responsible government.** Go to your local city council meetings and get a feel for the political conditions in you community. Go cause an uproar in your community by speaking out against inflated budgets. Be honest about your feelings and passionate in your delivery – this is your country – go protect it. Get your mayor and city council members worked into panic mode. Cause them to show their true colors by forcing them to expose themselves then let public opinion hang them on a political rope.

Threaten them with the prospect of not being re-elected. Beat them at their own game. Do what you need to do - in a peaceful way - to get them to listen to you. Force them to govern competently. Do not let them tune you out. Get in their face and protest the Tax Slavery that you have been subjected to. Do not let yourself become irrelevant. Politicians are completely disconnected from the economic reality of our basic conditions. The American Taxslaves are hurting terribly due to the political chaos that has been forced upon on us by our rulers that sit in untouchable seats of privilege.

"The liberties of a people never were or ever will be, secure when the transactions of their rulers may be concealed from them".

-Patrick Henry.

Can I ask you a question? Do you know your government? Honestly? I didn't think so. Ask anyone about the financial and economic health of our American Nation. You will get one of two responses. Taxpayers are not too thrilled. Tax consumers (social program recipients and government employee's) will tell you "life is good". Where does the money (funding) for social programs and government operation come from? It comes from the hard working American Taxslaves. Politicians tax us to the point of misery and destitution. Our rulers "legally" steal our earnings and spend it on useless government program that are based on false compassion - or the latest trend - "job creation" by way of short-lived public construction projects.

When did it become it the responsibility of our government to create jobs? I always thought that job creation was the responsibility of the

American people. Does the term "Free Market" sound familiar? Vivid examples of "tax and spend" politics in action are evident on all levels of government. A little trick used by politicians is "regulation". This is when federal and state governments force you- the taxpayer- to purchase a service of their choosing. Soon government will begin to impose "mandates" on the private sector by forcing us to buy a service from a corporation of their choice - one that meets the Federal requirements. The Federal Government will then step aside and claim, "This is not a tax". But, taxpayers know that if government requires the expenditure and they "guide" us to the provider of their choice, we as taxpayers only stand to lose. "Regulation" is an indirect tax that can create a whole new revenue source for government to feed from.

Our rulers continually deceive and trick us.

It is time to kick all of the unworthy men and women out of office. Men and women who will serve with integrity and honesty must replace them. Americans must hold their rulers accountable for their actions. Our economy is in trouble and our government is in trouble. Ultimately the American Taxslaves are in trouble. As a result, **America is facing a politically induced economic crisis.** It is time to live like responsible men and women and cut the waste of Big Government.

As of late 2009 the state of California had the 8th largest economy in the world at roughly 1.8 trillion dollars and was operating at a huge deficit. The state is on the borderline of bankruptcy. What does this tell us? It tells us that enough is enough. Taxpayers and more importantly, government must start to live within its means. Taxpayers can no longer represent a blank check. It is time to put the emergency brakes on! Our money is being wasted by ruthlessly ambitious men and women in office who promise to do things they cannot realistically do without breaking the economy and the taxpayer pockets. Big greedy government on all levels-city, county, state and federal is destroying America's future.

Is America still the land of opportunity? Are we still living in the most prosperous nation in the world?

It is estimated that more than 36 million out of 300 million Americans, (about 10% of people) purchase some of their food using food stamps.

Why is this?

There is enough potential and ability to create wealth in this country that we can all have the things that we want, need and desire. We simply have to put forth the effort to achieve it.

Government regulation and out of control government spending has us on the brink of economic disaster. The sad part is this - Americans are not even paying attention. Is this what America has become? Decade after decade we have proved that social program after social program has caused government spending to skyrocket. As a result of this, the American taxpayers are left to pay the bill. What do we have to show for the spending? Have we eliminated poverty, hunger and unemployment? No. Instead we have witnessed the destruction of the middle class and watched unimaginable debts stack up.

Government-enacted social programs cannot fix the problem. Only the free market can provide a solution. Unemployment, high taxes and an unresponsive government are the recipe for social and political disaster.

What is the solution? Our only option is to free the Taxslaves who represent the economic backbone of this country. They are the people who earn a living in the free market. The American Taxslaves must elect officials who are committed to reducing the tax burden that has been forcibly imposed on businesses. We must put forth the effort to implement a better tax structure that will encourage companies to hire employees while investing more money into developing and growing better products and more efficient services. We can start by breaking up the unions that hold corporations and various levels of government hostage. It would also be wise to put an end to government bailouts. Our rulers do not listen because we fail to speak out.

One of the primary motivating forces behind our economy is financial achievement. We want to earn so we spend money. Beware; spending can also be a very destructive force. See what will happen if you max out your credit card and fail to pay the bill – you can say goodbye to your assets and hello to the debt collector. The same thing happens when our government applies a "spend and spend more" approach to governing – "Goodbye economic freedom and hello Tax Slavery". We must be careful to make sure that we do not make ourselves even sicker from crippling effects of debt. It terrorizes me to such few people willing to speak out against Big Government and the tax burden that it imposes on the American Taxslaves. The average citizen fails to recognize what is really going on in the "ivory towers" of government. Excessive taxation and out of control government spending is destructive by nature. Debt is not healthy - especially government debt!

It is time for American taxpayers to implement a new plan - one that actually works. Taxpayers must work with as much coordination as possible to make this become a national movement. Although it must start at the local levels, we must not limit ourselves to local communities. The movement has already begun, as evident across the nation with the millions in attendance at the Tea Party rallies. The ultimate goal is a national movement. Go to your City Hall and protest high taxes. Speak out - make it a family event, invite neighbors and friends. Hold your own TEA Party - host your own town hall meeting with your neighbors and friends in your living room. Go out to your local city council meetings on a weekly basis. Make an effort to get five, ten, twenty or even a hundred people every week on the steps of your local City Hall. If taxpaying Americans show up consistently in big numbers we will see real change.

The disease of outrageous taxation is spreading. It is the responsibility of taxpaying Americans to administer the cure.

The simple laws of economics show us that when our economy shrinks, people do not spend money at the same rate as when economic growth occurs. This lack of spending causes government on all levels to take in less tax revenue. In an attempt to offset this, local governments pass the bill on to the taxpayers. As a result, the American Taxslaves are forced to make up the gap in the revenue deficit. **Government does not have a revenue problem - it has a spending problem.** We never hear government elected or appointed officials say "Let's cut the budget and spend less money". Why? Is it really that difficult to balance a budget? If taxpayers suggest service cuts, politicians respond with: "No cuts. Services are needed to preserve our communities". Really? Are the bloated salaries, benefits and pensions of public employee's necessary as well?

Ask the public service unions if their "mandated" raises are necessary in times of economic hardship. The local taxpayers (usually home-owners) are the ones forced to foot the bill for the political parasites who have found a way to milk the system. Tax hikes are common, and tax cuts are uncommon. We must put an end to this politically induced servitude sooner than later. The American Taxslaves must take matters into their own hands. Do your part and speak out! **We are writing the tale of American tyranny each day that we remain silent!**

Our freedom - especially economic freedom is not guaranteed. It was inherited by all generations since our separation from Britain. Freedom is something that each of us must work hard to maintain. We are only a generation away from becoming fully enslaved by taxes and Big Government. **We have no guarantee that our liberties will last indefinitely; it is not our birthright.** America's founding fathers will not rise from the ground to protect our liberties. Unfortunately, they are long gone. Thankfully for us, their instructions are not. The Declaration of Independence and our Constitution are still here – to be used as sacred resources for our use. They are the guidelines that will help us maintain our liberty and freedom. As Americans, we must study these words and live by them. It is up to each of us to embrace these values and keep them written in stone to pass on to future generations.

Freedom is important, so we must work to maintain it everyday - hang on to it like your life depends on it. Freedom is not a right of passage; instead it is something that must be earned on a day-to-day, week-to-week, month-to-month, year-to-year, election-to-election, and generation-to-generation basis. As Americans, the preservation of liberty is our national duty. We must maintain the freedom that has been handed to us. We cannot simply maintain it; we must cultivate it and protect it. Freedom must be enhanced and improved with each passing generation. Our current position of dependence is a result of years after year, and program after program of failure. Each level of government continues growing bigger and bigger with no end in sight. Americans are becoming more dependent on various levels of government to provide the services they need to simply exist. As it grows larger and larger, government has become more dependent on the earned income of the American Taxslaves - working taxpayers who provide money (earnings) - the fuel that supports and feeds the machine of Big Government. Americans have been tricked, and forced into funding public social programs through mistaken compassion.

In order to solve a problem, you must identify it for what it is (as it exists), in the applicable context. First you must identify the symptoms, how and where this problem exists in our individual lives? Is it beneficial or detrimental to each of us? Next we must come up with a plan to implement realistic solutions. We cannot be asked to keep throwing money at the problems caused by Big Government. The burden that taxpayers are required to bear only keeps growing worse and worse like an untreatable disease. Soon Big Government will consume us, if we do not do something to stop it in the early stages.

Tax increases cause taxpayers (and businesses) to stop spending money in other areas - like their local shops and businesses. Tax hikes cause us to tighten our belt buckles and stop making purchases that we would otherwise make that support our city and state economies. This is a driving force behind the reason why taxation directly affects our economy on both the local and national levels. High taxes on business directly affect employment in an adverse way - this also contributes to unemployment. Politicians are spending taxpayer earnings like Paris Hilton on a Fifth Avenue shopping spree. They have become tax-crazed spend-aholics. Forget about professional athletes, we need to drug test our politicians. They are spending us into economic servitude - not just out of our homes and communities, but also into Tax Slavery! Taxpayers are dying a slow and painful economic death. A stranger is in your home; the Big Bad Wolf is "huffing" and "puffing", ready to "blow your house down". He is standing at your front door and he is licking his lips. I refuse sit back and wait to be consumed. I am loading my "shotgun". I will politely and kindly ask the intruder to leave. If he refuses, I will take matters into my own hands. I suggest that all taxpayers do the same. **Your weapon (shotgun) is your vote.** (What? You thought I was calling for violence didn't you? No, we can and will to this peacefully).

Political activism is the most peaceful and effective way to overthrow an economically oppressive, tax addicted government. This must remain a peaceful and passionate movement. Americans must vote the right people into office. **If elected officials fail to be true public servants, it is up to us to throw them out.** It is time to raise the bar; do not settle for less than what you work for. Hard working taxpayers have a right to keep a greater portion of what they earn. **The right to live free is endowed by our Creator - not our government.**

We can secure the gift of economic freedom and independence by educating one another on the principles of true freedom. Each of us must take care of our own needs. Secure your independence from the wicked tax predators that are on the hunt for your hard earned income.

We are living in political denial. We deny the fact that government is used as a tool for corruption. Too many Americans believe that it is the responsibility of government to take care of us. It is time to wake up. We can no longer turn our heads and ignore the plain fact that we have become Taxslaves. Can anyone in government explain why it is impossible to balance a budget? There is no excuse for continuous overspending. Is this the best our political ruling class can do?

We must liberate the hard-working American Taxpayers.

Politicians have forced citizens to share their accomplished wealth so that the lazy, unmotivated portion of society can have things that they do not work for.

As hard working taxpayers, our backs have been pinned against the wall. The American Taxslaves have been backed into a corner - trapped with no way out. When an animal that feels threatened, it will bite you. Our taxpaying backs are against the wall. We have sharp teeth and we are ready to bite back.

We must train ourselves to become deadly ninjas in the art of tax protesting. Taxslaves need to master the art of putting the right people into office. **We must become 6th degree black belts in the art of "Tax-Must-Go".** Think back to the time of early civilizations when the caveman went out to hunt for his food and clubbed a dinosaur (or whatever it was we hunted back then) and returned to the cave with food for the cavewoman to prepare for dinner. I doubt that the "caveman city council" said "oh well, we know you went out and earned it, but, but we'll take it and re-distribute your dinner to society"…I can almost guarantee that the caveman would not allow that. He would have clubbed the "caveman city council" and had <u>them</u> for dinner. Because he went out and earned it with his bare hands, you can bet he was keeping it - for himself, his cavewoman, and his little cave baby. People still become vicious when their survival is at stake. The same thing must apply to us now. We are all cavemen looking to keep what is ours. We are still primitive in a sense; we have a basic survival instinct. Americans may have fancier amenities and more comfortable living conditions than in the early days of our existence, but at the end of each day we still need to keep what is ours so that we can ensure our own safety and economic security.

Abusive tax rates are damaging due to the fact that by its very nature, lends itself to the natural inclinations of men to "get more" the easy way. Most Americans understand the need and allow government to take some of our money (earnings) in order to provide necessary services. After all, some evils are necessary. However, government should serve a limited function in regard to caring for its citizens. The primary focus of government should be reduced to the protection of individuals from fire, violence, and natural disasters. In our case, government has overstepped its clearly defined boundaries. For example, politicians have created a "situation" for government sponsored affordable housing based on the fact that some people feel they "deserve" what they have not earned. This is called social engineering. Working taxpayers pay the bill for too many government run social programs.

This form of taxation is destructive and the fact that it has the power to divide and destroy our communities is clearly evident. Instead of working to "integrate" our communities based on racial and economic factors, our leaders need to "integrate" some common sense into their legislative process. Leave the rest up to hard work and sacrifice.

Each day we read and watch new stories of people losing their homes, a new business going under and families being ripped apart due to financial problems. Government regulation, taxes and overspending play the biggest role in our nation's economic demise. This is something that must be addressed whole-heartedly in a plain, honest manner. Until then, we need to start forcing our elected "leaders" to be responsible. Taxpayers must demand that the political chaos be stopped. Make your elected officials come to you - the taxpayer - with hat in hand, apologize and say, "We are going to fix this by reducing the size and scope of government". Roll your sleeves up and get to work. Make the decisions that your rulers refuse to make. Excessive taxes are poisonous because the political process is based on lies. Government taxation is destructive. Politicians jump through hoops to find legal ways to make us part with our earnings. They take taxpayers income and re-distribute it to those who have not earned it. If you are skeptical, and you find it hard to believe me, simply look at your next paycheck. How much is left for you? Look at all of your income, when you buy something, look at the receipt-how much did they take - again? Look at how much you are really taxed.

When you pay your property tax bill look at the amount you pay in the context of how much time it took you to earn. Once you do this, you will realize that you are a Taxslave and you are being bamboozled.

Politicians and government dependents (both working and non-working) are thieves and cowards running around acting as if they are compassionate. This is a blatant lie. The ruling class does not have our "best interests" in mind; they would not be terrorizing the American taxpayers if they did. On a daily basis, working Americans are being terrorized with government imposed economic servitude. It is time to use all of our resources and bond together to stop this tax madness. TAXSLAVES UNITE! We need to take our country and our liberty back from these greedy men and women who claim to be saviors to the working class. They are not saviors - they are oppressors. The more you pay in tax, the less disposable income you have. They build their wealth by confiscating yours. The ruling class has been hiding behind the false promises of "healthcare", "save the planet", "economic stimulation", "saving the American workers" and "too big to fail". Maybe I showed up to the party too late to enjoy the Cool-Aid, but it seems that everyone else is drunk and I am the only clear-headed person in the room. Our political rulers have sent the people of the United States into a frenzy of economic panic. "We the People" have followed along with wide eyes and a terribly damaging blind trust. "Gullible" is the best way to describe the "bailout" fever that has given Americans a terrible sense of "False Hope". Government bailouts are equivalent to an assault on our liberty. The American Taxslaves will ultimately pay for the bill of Big Government bailouts. If taxes are significantly cut, the additional money saved by individuals and business owners will be invested in some way. Companies will invest in themselves by creating new jobs. The average American people will buy property or goods. The ownership of private property is as fundamental to freedom as the Second Amendment is to individual safety. We are being taxed out of our ability to become financially secure. Many of us are unable to even attempt to accumulate wealth. Wealth re-distribution is preventing hard working Americans from laying their own economically secure foundation to build upon. We are so misguided - Americans are not stupid, so I cannot understand how we have fallen into this stupid thinking that international globalization and a socialized society is "good" for us. I work hard to get what I want. I do not work hard to give someone else what he or she wants. I do not put the priorities of foreign countries before the priorities of my own country. I care about my family, my friends, my neighbors, my city, my state, and my country - the United States of America.

I am not a citizen of the world - I am an American.

The political cash-grab must be stopped. It is up to us, not our rulers. Save your freedom, independence and your individual liberties. The American Taxslaves must fight against this oppressive government taxation. We must seek out other like-minded people who are willing to stand up and put an end to this forced economic servitude. The first battle you fight will be with yourself – break the chains of dependence on a ruling class. We are our government. For those of us who hope to reclaim true American independence we have one option - fight. We must rise to the challenge just as generations of Americans in the past have done. It is now our time to serve. The Taxslave Revolution has already started. State by state, we are already economically enslaved by our rulers- in financially mandated shackles. Now is the time to break free. "We the People" must do it together.

Our ammunition is powerful – it is our voice and our vote.

Taxpayers must become individual tyrants; monarchs who are willing to govern their own lives and rule with an iron fist. Each of us must regulate our own personal "kingdoms". We must rule government with a firm hand. American citizens can no longer accept a top down government. A smaller government that works from the bottom up is essential to the preservation of these United States. Government must answer to the taxpayers because without us there is no money (wealth) to go around. Big Government needs taxpayers more than we need them. **It is time for the American**

Taxslaves to unify. Taxpayer unity is crucial to this movement and is something that must happen if we want to be successful. Taxpayers must remember these words: "United we stand, divided we fall".

Cities across this country that were once prosperous centers of economic prosperity have become ghost towns. Jobs have been outsourced to emerging economies because overseas corporations can produce goods and provide service at a cheaper rate than we do. Government regulation has devastated our production capacity. Emerging economies are infamous for cheaper labor, fewer government restrictions, and less oppressive taxation. Common sense must once again be applied to American business. Our government penalizes American companies for moving overseas in search of cheap labor. So, make no mistake about it - the American people pay the taxes for big corporations. They simply roll the tax burden into the cost of the product in order to maximize their profits.

The profit motive does not make a corporation evil. It is actually government-imposed taxation and regulatory interference that represent the greatest malice towards to our economy. Corporations simply "pass the buck" to the consumers. In reality, the so-called "evil" corporations are only acting like indirect tax collectors. This is a form of indirect taxation imposed on the consumers by the tax terrorizing members of our government.

Capitalism is an effective system when government does not destroy it. Our rulers need to stop "villainizing" Capitalism and place the blame where it belongs -on out of control politicians. Taxation and government regulation are evils that send companies packing in search of overseas markets that will allow for greater economic prosperity. **Big Government and taxation are both oppressive by nature and both have led to the current Tax Tyranny we are forcibly subjected to.** Our ruling class has a stranglehold on the American Taxslaves. The American people have been sentenced to carry the economic burdens that many failed political policies have created.

We must remove the evil of Big Government from our shores. **Our rulers have destroyed the American Dream.** It is one thing to do your part as a taxpayer, but providing for the needs of other fully capable people who choose not to get up and be productive members of society is not acceptable. Why does our own government encourage confiscation of our earnings? It is time to get these rulers out of our way. Government is needed for basic essentials like safety, security and disaster response. Overall, our political class should be limited in almost every other capacity.

It is an abuse of government power when as taxpayers, we are required to break our backs in order to fund the tax consuming part of society - those who live off of our hard work, our effort and our sacrifice.

Each one of us must become an weapon of liberty and work tirelessly to free our American Republic from the grip of economic enslavement. You cannot be a silent weapon - you must make noise. This will not be an easy battle; it will be an uprising of angry Tax Peasants filled with emotions and fiery passion. We can reclaim our dignity from the hands of the ruling class that is responsible for taking it from us. Redistribution of our wealth and a significant portion of our earnings is no longer an option for us. Our country is on the edge of the cliff - the brink of financial ruin, and it is a long way down. Are you ready and willing to fight and stand your ground? Will you fight to maintain safe economic ground under your feet? Or, will you allow yourself to be bullied along until you are pushed off the cliff and fall into further economic enslavement?

The choice is ours to make. The deciding factor in this battle for American independence will be our actions – rely on yourself – not your government.

There is an evil wave of Socialist thinking consuming people, and it is right outside of our door. We cannot wait for someone else to save us. Our elected "leaders" will not come rescue us - so take the initiative, and build your own local movement. Take pride in the fact that you are fighting to keep what you earn. You are not begging for a handout – instead you are demanding to keep more of what your time, effort, expertise, and hard work produces. Big Government will lead to the ultimate consumption of your time and your earnings. Total control of the time, effort and wealth of the people is equivalent to centralized government control – Communism. I work for my own interests - not the interests of our state and federal rulers. I get up and I go to work. As a result, I demand to keep what I earn. I make this demand because I am the one motivated enough to go to work for it. My earnings must not be taken from me under the false pretense of "compassion". I work for my own needs, not the needs of my neighbors.

Big Government will be the ultimate destruction of American taxpayers and personal liberty. Our freedoms are being stripped under the disguise of compassion. The wolf is hiding among us in sheep's clothing. Politicians promise to spend more money on programs and services, but also promise to cut taxes. They are genuinely out of touch. We are fools for following along with the political poisoning of our minds. Our governments (local, state and federal) have become soft tyrannies that are hardening every day. It is time for us to smack each other in the head and say, "wake the heck up".

America is on fire – if we hope to save it we cannot run for the exit, we must stand and fight the flames. If each American Taxslave stands defiant and fights the blaze, our house will still be standing in the morning. I will burn down with this house before I run!

I cannot think of a system of governing that is more detrimental to a "free" country than the one we are currently subjected to. Fascists and Communists clearly express their desire for central planning and state control. Our rulers hide it under the disguise of "compassion" and "change".

We have a system where government taxes its citizens (actually only taxpayers) at a rate greater than fifty percent. I cannot understand how many Americans still believe we are free. The next section includes a "short" list of taxes levied (imposed) on us by our elected rulers. Enjoy.

List of Taxes paid by Americans:

(Source: www.electivedecisions.wordpress.com)

1. Accounts Receivable Tax
2. Accounting and Tax Preparation (cost to taxpayers $300 billion)
3. Accumulated Earnings Tax
4. Accumulation Distribution of Trusts
5. Activity Fee (Dumping Permit Fee)
6. Air Tax (PA coin-operated vacuums)
7. Aircraft Jet Fuel Tax
8. Aircraft Excise Tax
9. Alcohol Fuels Tax
10. Alcoholic Beverage Tax
11. Alternative Minimum Tax – Amt
12. Ambulance Services (Air Ambulance Services, SD)
13. Ammunition Tax
14. Amusement Tax (MA, VA, MD)
15. Animal Slaughter Tax (WI, others, Per Animal)
16. Annual Custodial Fees (Ira Accounts)
17. Ballast Water Management Fee (Marine Invasive Species)
18. Bio-diesel Fuel Tax
19. Blueberry Tax (Maine)

20. Bribe Taxes (Pay If You Dare)

21. Brothel licensing fees

22. Building Permit Tax

23. Capital Gains Tax

24. California Interstate User Diesel Fuel Tax

25. California Redemption Value (Can and Bottle Tax)

26. CDL License Tax

27. Charter Boat Captain License

28. Childhood Lead Poisoning Prevention Fee

29. Cigarette Tax

30. Cigarette Tax Stamp (Acts) (Distributors)

31. Compressed Natural Gas Tax

32. Commercial Activity Tax (OH – for Service Providers)

33. Corporate Income Tax

34. Court Fines (Indirect Taxes)

35. County Property Tax

36. Disposable Diapers Tax (Wisconsin)

37. Disposal Fee (Any Landfill Dumping)

38. Dog License Tax

39. Duck Hunting Tax Stamp (PA, others)

40. Electronic Waste Recycling Fee (E-Waste)

41. Emergency Telephone User Surcharge

42. Environmental Fee (CA – Haz-Mat Fees)

43. Estate Tax (Death Tax, to be reinstated)

44. Excise Taxes

45. Facility Fee (CA – Haz-Mat Fees)

46. FDIC tax (insurance premium on bank deposits)

47. Federal Income Tax

48. Federal Unemployment Tax (FUTA)

49. Fiduciary Income Tax (Estates and Trusts)

50. Fishing License Tax

51. Flush Tax (MD Tax For Producing Wastewater)

52. Food License Tax

53. Fountain Soda Drink Tax (Chicago – 9%)

54. Franchise Tax

55. Fresh Fruit (CA, if Purchased From A Vending Machine)

56. Fuel Gross Receipts Tax (Retail/Distributor)

57. Fuel Permit Tax

58. Fur Clothing Tax (MN)

59. Garbage Tax

60. Gasoline Tax (475 Cents Per Gallon)

61. Generation-Skipping Transfer Tax

62. Generator Fee (Recycled Waste Fee)

63. Gift Tax

64. Gross Receipts Tax

65. Habitat Stamp (Hunting/Fishing in some states)

66. Hamburger Tax

67. Hazardous Substances Fees: Generator, Facility, and Disposal

68. Highway Access Fee

69. Household Employment Taxes

70. Hunting License Tax

71. Illegal Drug Possession (No Carolina)

72. Individual Income Tax

73. Inheritance Tax

74. Insect Control Hazardous Materials License

75. Insurance Premium Tax

76. Intangible Tax (Leases Of Govt. Owned Real Property)

77. Integrated Waste Management Fee

78. Interstate User Diesel Fuel Tax

79. Inventory Tax

80. IRA Rollover Tax (a transfer of IRA money)

81. IRA Early Withdrawal Tax

82. IRS Interest Charges

83. IRS Penalties (Tax On Top Of Tax)

84. Jock Tax (income earned by athletes in some states)

85. Kerosene, Distillate, & Stove Oil Taxes

86. Kiddie Tax (Child's Earned Interest Form 8615)

87. Land Gains and Real Estate Withholding

88. Lead Poisoning Prevention Fee (Occupational)

89. Lease Severance Tax

90. Library Tax

91. Liquid Natural Gas Tax

92. Liquid Petroleum Gas Tax

93. Liquor Tax

94. Litigation Tax (TN Imposes Varies With the Offense)

95. LLC/PLLC Corporate Registration Tax

96. Local Income Tax

97. Lodging Taxes

98. Lump-Sum Distributions

99. Luxury Taxes

100. Make-Up Tax (Ohio, applying in a salon is taxable)

101. Marriage License Tax

102. Meal Tax

103. Medicare Tax

104. Mello-Roos Taxes (Special Taxes and Assessments)

105. Migratory Waterfowl Stamp (addition to hunting license)

106. Minnow Dealers License (Retail – For One Shop)

107. Minnow Dealers License (Distributor – For One+ Shops)

108. Mobile Home Ad Valorem Taxes

109. Motor Fuel Tax (For Suppliers)

110. Motor Vehicle Tax

111. Music and Dramatic Performing Rights Tax

112. Nudity Tax (Utah)

113. Nursery Registration (Buying and selling plants)

114. Occupancy Inspection Fees

115. Occupation Taxes and Fees (Various Professional Fees)

116. Oil and Gas Assessment Tax

117. Oil Spill Response, Prevention, and Administration Fee

118. Parking Space Taxes

119. Pass-Through Withholding

120. Pay-Phone Calls Tax (Indiana)

121. Percolation Test Fee

122. Personal Property Tax

123. Personal Holding Company (undistributed earnings)

124. Pest Control License

125. Petroleum Business Tax

126. Playing Card Tax (Al)

127. Pole Tax (TX – A $5 Cover Charge On Strip Clubs)

128. Profit from Illegal Drug Dealing

129. Property Tax

130. Property Transfer Tax (DE, ownership transfer between parties)

131. Prostitution Tax (NV – Prostitute Work Permits)

132. Poultry Registered Premises License (Sales License)

133. Rain Water Tax (Runoff after a Storm)

134. Rat Control Fee (CA)

135. Real Estate Tax

136. Recreational Vehicle Tax

137. Refrigerator and Freezer Recycling Fees

138. Regional Transit Taxing Authority (Trains)

139. Road Usage Tax

140. Room Tax (Hotel Rooms)

141. Sales Tax (State)

142. Sales Tax (City)

143. Sales And Use Tax (Sellers Permit)

144. School Tax

145. Service Charge Tax

146. Self-Employment Tax

147. Septic And Drain Field Inspection Fees

148. Sex Sales Tax (UT, when nude people perform services)

149. Sewer & Water Tax

150. Social Security Tax

151. Sparkler and Novelties Tax (WV Sellers of Sparklers, etc)

152. Special Assessment Tax (Not Ad Valorem)

153. State Documentary Stamp Tax on Notes (FL RE Tax)

154. State Franchise Tax

155. State Income Tax

156. State Park Fees

157. State Unemployment Tax (SUTA)

158. Straight Vegetable Oil (SVO) Fuel Tax

159. Stud Fees (Kentucky's Thoroughbred Sex Tax)

160. Tangible Personal Property Tax

161. Tattoo Tax (AR Tax On Tattoos)

162. Telephone 911 Service Tax (some states)

163. Telephone Federal Excise Tax

164. Telephone Federal Universal Service Fee Tax

165. Telephone Federal Surcharge Taxes

166. Telephone State Surcharge Taxes

167. Telephone Local Surcharge Taxes

168. Telephone Minimum Usage Surcharge Tax

169. Telephone Recurring Charges Tax

170. Telephone Universal Access Tax

171. Telephone Non-Recurring Charges Tax

172. Telephone State Usage Charge Tax

173. Telephone Local Usage Charge Tax

174. Tire Recycling Fee

175. Tobacco Tax (Cigar, Pipe, Consumer Tax)

176. Tobacco Tax (Cigar, Pipe, Dealer Tax)

177. Toll Road Taxes

178. Toll Bridge Taxes

179. Toll Tunnel Taxes

180. Tourism or Concession License Fee

181. Traffic Fines (Indirect Taxation)

182. Transportable Treatment Unit Fee (Small Facility)

183. Trailer Registration Tax

184. Trout Stamp (Addendum To Fish License)

185. Use Taxes (On Out-Of-State Purchases)

186. Utility Taxes

187. Unemployment Tax

188. Underground Storage Tank Maintenance Fee

189. Underpayment of Estimated Tax (Form 2210)

190. Unreported Tip Income (Social Security and Medicare Tax)

191. Vehicle License

192. Vehicle Recovery Tax (CO, to find stolen cars)

193. Vehicle Registration Tax

194. Vehicle Sales Tax

195. Wagering Tax (Tax on Gambling Winnings)

196. Waste Vegetable Oil (WVO) Fuel Tax

197. Water Rights Fee

198. Watercraft Registration Tax

199. Waterfowl Stamp Tax

200. Well Permit Tax

201. Wiring Inspection Fees

202. Workers Compensation Tax

Are you still under their spell?

I challenge you to figure it out for yourself. Identify the real calculation of what you spend on taxes. That money (percent of your earned income) can and should go towards growing your own wealth and economic security. Unfortunately, it does not. Instead, it is forcibly taken from you (the taxpayer) then re-distributed, and "handed out" to voting blocks of dependents and public employee unions who feel entitled to your earnings. Now wait, I forgot that government employees do work for a living - just take a walk down to your local Department of Motor Vehicles and you can see their hard work on display. Go get a look at all the hard work you see going on there. Unfortunately for us they are grossly overpaid in both salary and benefits. We have government employees on all levels making a fine living off of our hard work – our tax dollars – our forced labor!

The majority of public employees (not all) are living off of our hard work. These tax consumers want what true free market taxpayer's work hard for. Because these tax consumers make up a huge voting block, they get what they demand. They get the economic benefits of our hard work. The cause of this is unbridled government spending, which inevitably leads to higher levels of taxation. As a result of this, our ability to provide for ourselves is degraded. Budgets on all levels of government are exploding at the seams. Union leaders demand more for their members - this means less for the homeowners, or the aspiring homeowners. In my home city of New Rochelle (a New York suburb roughly fifteen minutes north of Manhattan) - it costs home owning taxpayers over $ 22, 000.00 a year per for public education. Why? This prevents taxpaying American homeowners from keeping what we earn. This damages our ability to achieve various goals, like starting our own business, or retiring after working twenty, thirty or forty years without having to worry about eating cat food for dinner. I know this statement is a little extreme, but you can understand my point.

One of the duties of higher office- senate, congress, or president- is to protect us – the American people – from all threats, foreign or domestic. One of the major domestic threats to "We the People" is government spending - because it leads to the forced confiscation of out earnings.

Government spending is the biggest threat to our financial independence.

Politicians are sworn into office with the duty to protect us. Unfortunately, they are actuality the main culprits behind our misery. Economically reckless legislators will lead to the ultimate destruction of the American taxpayers. They are grabbing onto our back while we tirelessly try to stay afloat. These are the same people who threw our economic lifeboats overboard. American Taxslaves are subjected to a political ruling class that seeks to control every aspect of our lives. Look at the financial burden the taxpayers are forced to bear at the hands of our elected officials. Government forces too much responsibility on the taxpaying portion of society. For example, un-funded mandates, affordable housing and government provided pensions are wasteful tools used to gain votes for election and re-election.

If our politicians want us to serve their purpose and protect the American people from external threats like 9/11 attacks, they must also and just as importantly, protect us from internal threats like the progressive-ultra liberal left who seek to re-distribute our wealth and de-stabilize our economy It is necessary to address the issue of abusive taxation for what it is - legalized theft and forced economic servitude.

It is sad to know that one of the primary political facts of life is that incumbents always seek re-election and do it by using any means necessary. One clever trick is their passage of legislation that will increase our taxes to provide services for segments of our society that do not earn it. Ruthless politicians promise to pass legislation that will re-distribute earned wealth to the poor and unfortunate simply because they make up the greater voting block in a political district – this does not serve the best interests of

America or the taxpayers of this nation. The facts of political life are not always based on honesty, truth and integrity. The goal of our political class is simply re-election - not integrity, not non-interference, not rule of law, not freedom, and not independence. Instead, their focus is on one thing - the power of political office. The focus of all public servants should be on maintaining the character of our communities and our country. Our leaders must work to keep the opportunity to achieve the American dream alive. **The majority our politicians focus on gaining and holding on to political power. In the game of "rule over men", this has always been and will always be. Therefore we must rise up and challenge our rulers by removing them from our American political system.**

We must re-establish our Constitutional Republic.

American taxpayers (the Taxslaves) must rise up and launch a political "witch hunt" just like they did in Salem, Massachusetts. But, rather than burning the culprits at a stake, we need to burn them at the voting booths. Let's launch a devastating manhunt to filter out the wolves in sheep's clothing that are hiding inside of our government.

Incumbents, appointed officials and all of the other political fools that have dragged this country to the brink of to financial ruin are the main culprits. We must target the greedy, power hungry traitors who are damaging our lives, stealing our earnings and confiscating our economic property.

An American Fall from Grace

Do Americans still have an identity? What do we stand for? What are we proud of? Are we living off the achievements of past generations of free men and women? Are we really the spoiled, unappreciative, materialistic, self-indulgent people that the rest of the world thinks we are? Perhaps, but it is because generation after generation of Americans have sacrificed and improved - getting better, smarter and more productive with each passing generation. Countless resources and technological innovations have allowed us to be this way. Perhaps we deserve it. We are reaping the benefits of what many, many great Americans worked for and passed on to us. What are we doing with our opportunity? Despite the current economic downturn, Americans have not been forced to deal with a devastating tragedy over a prolonged period of time - like a World War, a Great Depression or the threat of nuclear annihilation at any given moment. We've had it pretty easy for nearly a quarter of a century. September 11th was terrible for all Americans, so I do not mean to minimize the devastating impact, but thank God most people watched it happen on television and were not subjected to the terror of being there in person - may God rest every Soul that perished. From the ashes we will grow stronger. Our spirits are down, but America's soul will not be broken.

Too many of us fail to realize how blessed we truly are. Even though we fail sometimes, we have more to be proud of than ashamed of. Failure is helpful because it makes us better and wiser. Individuals and corporations must be allowed to fail. Economies have failed, businesses have crumbled and people have lost their fortunes before - this is not a new concept.

Americans have recovered before and we will rebuild once again. Failures will happen again and again, but we will recover as long as we keep our instinct to survive sharp.

American citizens are lucky to have a quality of life that could have never been imagined only a half a century ago. We have food, clothing, entertainment, and security unprecedented in any other time in history. We have this because preceding generations of Americans have stood defiant in the face of each challenge that threatened to damage our great nation. The strength and courage of generations past were tested, and they rose to the occasion successfully each time they were asked to - out of necessity. Plan "B" was to re-enforce Plan "A"…Remain Free.

We began as a nation of explorers and entrepreneurs who ended up becoming the envy of the world - not only for what we have, but also for all the good we have done for the human race. America has defined a new type of success. No other country of politically and economically oppressed people in the course of civilized history has ever come close to doing what we did in the past 234 years. America has conquered many life threatening diseases that previously devastated continents from shore to shore, advanced the cause of liberty, successfully ended two world wars, sent a man to the moon and freed the soul of man to dream bigger than he ever imagined possible. I am proud to call myself an American!

Our American predecessors did not allow themselves to become dependent or lazy – they had a survival instinct that we lack today. Our comfort has softened us to the point that we even refuse to fight off our own elected leaders from over stepping well-established social and political boundaries. **Economic disasters, external threats and civil unrest here at home have not broken the will or spirit of the American people – and it will not now.**

Success is not guaranteed simply because we are Americans. We must accept the fact that life is not always fair and realize that bad things do happen. America is what it is today because "We the People" worked hard and sacrificed for it. Americans have always resisted oppression, and fought back against all dangers that threatened them. It is now our turn to rise to the challenges facing us. We must apply wisdom and strength to our actions if we hope to win this fight. Our goal is to remove all of the oppressive tax-obsessed rulers from public office. They are obstructing our progress towards freedom, individual liberty and a restoration of our Constitutional Republic.

It has become acceptable for us to look to our government when times get difficult. This is not what free, self-reliant people do. Unfortunately, government has a problem saying "no" to potential votes and will turn to taxpayers when times get difficult (tax hikes). I suggest that as taxpayers we cut out the middleman and rely on ourselves. We should look to each other for encouragement and support – not our government. Let me repeat this - we do not need Big Government, we can do things on our own!

Governments are made up of men, and as history proves, men will never release control once they have it. We must strip away the power of our political class. Our determination to succeed will help us achieve our goal of restoring individual liberty, public accountability and true freedom.

A clear plan on how to achieve our goal does not exist. Each of us must find our own way to contribute what we can. Our first step is to get the political ruling class out of our way. It is necessary to vote them out of office so that we can plan a future as free men and women. Government has confiscated taxpayer money to fund everything from welfare and food stamps to public education and "fair" housing in order to "help" people that are in a "false" state of "need". Now, it is the taxpayers that need help. We need relief. We must force the hand of Big Government out of our pockets and it's nose out of our business! Independence and self-reliance will be difficult for some people to adjust to, but we must encourage them to stand up unsupported by anything other than their own work ethic and ability. The things that challenge us the most are also the things that bring out the best in us. If independence and success were easily achieved would they be worth fighting for? Living a life free from any dominating influence is what makes life worthwhile.

We have two choices; live free or bow down. Independence requires us to be self-reliant. Self-reliance starts with a change in attitude. Transform your thoughts from "I won't" to "I will" - from "I do not know how to" to "I will figure it out" - from "I can't" to "I did". Achievement and failure are both the result of a specific state of mind. By working through our worst challenges we virtually guarantee that better days will come. You must have the heart and confidence in yourself to know that even when seemingly insurmountable odds are stacked against you, you can maintain independence through hard work and determination. Americans are durable – we refuse to crumble under the pressure of hopeless moments that challenge to devastate our soul.

Through perseverance and commitment to unity we can build confidence and define the character of our nation once again.

Devastating challenges are what have always united the people of our American nation. We are capable of achieving so many great, positive and amazing things in our lifetime if we only put in the time and effort required. By achieving independence once again, we will truly become free from self-imposed limitations that have constrained us from being the best that we can be. Only when we are self-reliant will we be able to understand what it means to be free. This will happen when we fight for, and realize self-government. Encourage your friends and neighbors to live free from political and economic oppression. Make sure you are responsible for your own actions and your future. If you know someone who is dependent on government or anyone else, challenge him or her to break the addiction. Show support and help them reach their ability to attain real freedom.

Some people really do need public assistance - and that is fine - if, and only if it is an absolute necessity. Eventually the time comes for people to release the grip from the hand of government and provide for their own needs.

We must have a burning desire to live like free men and women. Otherwise we will continue to live like slaves - Taxslaves who serve their government rulers and provide for their "capable" neighbors.

Big Government is like the Serpent, encouraging us to eat the apple that fell from the poisonous Tree of Dependence.

Members of our political ruling class have become architects of deceit and as a result, the American taxpayers have become Taxslaves! It is time to get off the couch and rebel against the Tax Terrorists that threaten our American independence.

Social programs waste taxpayer dollars. **The earned income of the working class has become the fuel for laziness and dependence.** Government handouts are only meant to bridge the gap for a small percentage of legal Americans that have been hit by hard times. Public assistance is only meant to assist them until they get back on their feet. The purpose is to bridge the gap, not to encourage a lifestyle of dependence. Too many people have abused our political system over long periods of time. It breaks my heart to know that Big Government has enslaved so many Americans. Dependence on government is a waste of potential and a waste of our tax dollars. **Social welfare programs have done more damage to the people of our country than any foreign power has ever done. Welfare is a tool of political enslavement.** Americans should never take assistance from the government unless it means the difference between life and death. If you depend on government for your needs I suggest that you get off the assistance as fast as you can. It is our duty as Americans and as free men to reject that kind of unacceptable lifestyle. Free men should never rely on their government to provide for them – they must rely on their own abilities. If we become dependent on a body of government we cease to be free. Those that live in a state of need have become subjects to a ruling class. We must make sure that we live within our means as individuals and as a nation.

I refuse to be enslaved to any system of government, especially my own. A life lived in "need" is a life lived enslaved. Refuse to live in political and economic debt - because you will eventually be forced to obey your master.

If we remain on our current path, the crash of our economic system is inevitable. If this happens, "We the People" will be responsible for rebuilding it - not our government.

We have a duty to protect the freedom that was passed on to us by our founders. Our American Republic came with an owner's manual - the Constitution. If you are ready to give up your freedom instead of fighting for independence then you do not deserve to call yourself an American. When our time in history passes, we will either be standing proud or kneeling down in shame. The choice is ours to make. Live your life free from tax oppression and dependence on a ruling class. I speak out because I choose to live like a free man. Understand what independence is and then live it. A free existence is the only meaningful life. Dependence is a miserable and meaningless existence.

We can take the stress and the economic burden off of ourselves if we remove government waste of our earnings and government dependents from the voting booths.

The best and quickest way to fix our Republic is to implement a single rule - if you do not pay taxes you should not be able to vote! The right to vote should always be there for each one of us, but we must earn the ability to add our "two cents" when it comes to elections. We can only force accountability in government by preventing people who do not

earn tax dollars from having a say in how our tax dollars are spent. Political bribery should have no place in our society.

We need to lower our taxes and force people to provide for their own interests. We cannot look to government to provide for anything other than what we openly delegate it to provide. Because our elected officials forcibly impose economic destitution upon us, it is our duty to remove the problem. We can achieve this by voting for men and women who seek to be true public servants. Taxpaying American citizens must encourage people to run for office that have the heart and courage to cut budgets, reduce the size of government and minimize state and federal handouts to people who are capable of going out and earning a living on their own. People must provide for their own needs - prosperity must not be the role of government. It is not the duty of a free people to give up control of their lives to their government. It is in our nature to endure and survive. Successful communities will leave no room for full time dependence on government. It is time to force people to find a way to earn a of living on their own - not at the expense of others who have their own families and individual needs to tend to.

Reliance on government for employment, "free" money, "free" food, "free" housing and "free" education is unacceptable. People will find a way to live free from Big Government assistance if they are forced to. We need to remove government from the equation and remind ourselves that as Americans, we are capable of doing great things on our own. Now is the time to prevent government-intervention in our economic lives. If we took the profits of each of the "Fortune Five Hundred" companies, for the next 145 years we would have enough money to pay off the current national debt. Change is badly needed. We must force our government officials and legislators to cut the massive spending. The spending habits of our ruling class must change. This is change we can believe in. Anything less will lead to sure economic destruction.

Take a look at the Trillions of dollars of debt that our government has piled on us. Is this what a free citizen works for? Do you work to pay the tab for Big Government spending? Taxpayer dollars pay the interest on our national debt - which is an astronomical number. Very few elected officials will even discuss this - let alone propose a solution. When the free market is left alone to create the products that people need, at a fair price, America will prosper. Instead, Capitalism is being "villainized". Capitalism is not the cause of our economic problems – the problems have been caused by the restrictions placed on the free market by Big Government. Big Government is the villain, not Capitalism. Our greatest economic achievements have come from the free market - not government.

When Americans have no food on the table they will learn the value of hard work and learn to be resourceful – my Grandfather taught me this. He learned it the hard way during the Great Depression. People must find a way to make their lives worthwhile. Government handouts have suffocated our survival instincts. By being all things to all people, government officials are enslaving the working class of America. Desperate people will allow themselves to be enslaved in order to survive. People will sacrifice their freedom and security for survival. **Let's break the cycle of dependence on our political rulers. We are moving closer to becoming a culture of total dependence.** America is turning into a society of controlled citizens. Although we may not want to admit it, we must realize that it is indeed happening and we must do something to fix the problem.

Our money (economic income) is our means of survival, and we are being stripped of it because of government spending. Our ruling class has an unquenchable thirst for our earnings because they make a never-ending amount of promises. This is a result of their quest for election and re-election to political office.

The American Taxslaves must hunt down the Tax Terrorists who are responsible for the current system of economic enslavement and wealth re-distribution. It is time to expose the people who created this mess. We must cast the power hungry ruling class out of our government and our society. They are traitors to liberty and freedom. We must to do this with an open and honest government that is truly "Of the people, by the people and for the people." Real change will only come when we put open and honest officials in office that will echo the real voice of the independent American people.

Our elected and appointed rulers are spending billions of our tax dollars overseas in an attempt to hunt down those who are a threat to the United States. Just as importantly, we also need to have a large army of taxpayers here at home, hunting down those responsible for the Big Government, spend-crazy Tax Terrorists here at home.

We see and hear commercials all the time for crazy things like artificial appetite suppressors. Advertisers tell us "You are too fat…take this pill and it will suppress your appetite … you'll lose weight because you will not crave as much food as you normally do".

I have a better idea, let's implement an appetite suppression pill for government. We are the capsules. We are the "suppressant" that must curb government's excessive appetite for spending our economic property. **Just as sure as overeating will make us fat, overspending will make us broke.** This applies to both individuals and to our nation as a whole. It is the responsibility of taxpaying Americans to curb government's appetite for our earned income. We the taxpayers are the "dietary supplement" that can put an end to the "fatness" of government. Lets put our government on a spending diet.

Our elected officials viewed the Tea Party rallies and the town hall meetings as an inconvenience. Why were we an inconvenience to them? They were put in office to represent the voice of the people. **The function of elected officials is simple - represent the will the taxpaying people and enforce the law of the land – the Constitution.**

Our elected "leaders" must remember that they were put into office to represent our voices. We elect them to serve us, and echo our wants, needs, and desires - not theirs. It is time for our "rulers" to do what we put them in office to do - represent the taxpayers. Point your finger in the face of the rulers and say "DON'T TREAD ON US"! Stop spending our hard earned money. Fed up taxpayers are not the burden, the reckless spend-aholics in government are the menace. Our elected "leaders" were elected to office by the people to serve a purpose - to preserve a free society and protect our freedom and independence. Instead, they threaten us with further economic enslavement. Our leaders in both Washington and our local communities have failed to do their job.

The recent, grassroots TEA Party movements have been called things like "Astro-Turf" and its members are called "Town Hall Terrorists". Elected officials have done everything in their power to avoid face-to-face meetings. Some have gone so far as to set up impersonal Internet based cyber-meetings - anything to avoid meeting with their constituents. They did not want to "catch the heat" of the taxpayers. **Our elected officials are Tax Terrorists.** By hitting us hard in the pockets and then hiding out like Bin Laden in the "cave" of cyber space they have damned themselves to live in political limbo. The so-called "Town Hall Terrorists" that attended meetings were American taxpayers and homeowners who were justifiably angry because they felt like their elected officials were not listening to them. They were right nobody was listening. We have their attention now. Even though some meetings got out of hand - people began yelling, and screaming - there has been absolutely no violence - only a passionate movement towards liberty and speaking out against an encroaching system of Tax Slavery. This is what our elected officials must be forced to deal with if they fail to perform true public service. It is their responsibility to bear the brunt of angry taxpayers. My advice to them, "take your medicine like a big boy…if you can't take the heat then get the heck out of the kitchen". After all, as taxpayers, we are the ones who have to bear the brunt of writing out tax checks for wasteful government programs and reckless legislation. We need to surgically implant responsible people into government. Forced responsibility will be the only way to minimize the consumption of our tax dollars by an out of touch political class.

We must force our "leaders" to cut the spending and cut the waste. Unless drastic spending cuts are made, our elected officials will continue to feel the wrath of the Taxslaves. In the interest of liberty, we must continue to give them an earful at town hall meetings. If they still refuse to listen, we must serve them with walking papers on Election Day. "We the People" must force them to live up to their responsibility as elected representatives of the people. This is only the beginning of the Taxslave Revolution…this is only the beginning.

Our ruling class will feel the pressure if they continue to betray and undermine our efforts to live life free and independent of political oppression. I cannot wait until Election Day - our rulers will feel the wrath of the economically enslaved taxpayers. The time is coming and the reign of Big Government will soon come to an end. A new Age of Political Enlightenment is overtaking the American taxpayers. The voting block of taxpayers will, if we effectively unify, put excessive government spending to an abrupt end. You can bet your re-election on that!

The economic enslavement we are facing is self-imposed because we did not take the time out of our busy schedules to learn what the proper role of government is in our lives. For far too long we have failed to elect the right people to office. For generations we have failed to hold the people we did put into office accountable for their poor decisions and economically damaging actions. Because of our indifference in regard to our political process, we are now literally paying the price for our own failure. If our entire economic system collapses tomorrow, we will be able to recover. Our indomitable spirit is the core of American greatness. This is not only something that we read about in books or learn in school. Instead, it is something in our spirit that is inherent in our human nature- the will to survive. We can survive and prosper without Big Government. Political parties do not matter – each of us must live responsible lives. We must not expect to be "bailed out" by our government. The most important ingredient in our lives must be freedom. Freedom requires us to be independent and embrace individual responsibility.

As Americans, we must live with "self government" as the foundation of our lives. It is our responsibility as free men and women to embrace personal accountability, freedom, independence, and personal achievement. We cannot give in to the idea that government must take care of our needs.

As Americans, we must work hard, make smart financial decisions and protect ourselves from ever having to depend on someone else for our existence. It is our responsibility to make sure that we do not create a system of government control that is too big to escape from. Smart economic decisions in our own personal lives will help ensure financial safety and security. Living smart and within our means will provide the protection we need to maintain a free existence. **How can you call a man free if a governing body has legislative, political and economic dominance over him?** Your time and effort must never be "owned" by your government.

I have a great idea for a reality show. Let's take a city or a town government (city council, legislators, etc…) and put them on television in a "political reality show". Cameras can follow them around and focus on them 24/7- just like MTV's "Real World" or "Jersey Shore". The ultimate goal should be to have them cut the budget by 50 percent. I would love to watch their struggle. Most taxpayers would like to see the things they will do to attempt to balance a budget - put their actions on display for everyone to see. If the goal of cutting a budget by 50 percent is achieved, they will instantly be propelled into the national political spotlight. They will become instant celebrities - political "rock stars". That is an idea that will hold its weight in gold.

I hope someone out there is crazy enough to undertake a project like this. I am eager to see how it would turn out.

Governments on all levels are piling tax obligations on to an already heavily burdened tax paying population. Our budgets are too big. We need politicians that will both change and improve – if not, they should be removed from public office.

It is our duty to restore strength to the leaders in our government. We can no longer accept weakness when it comes to the leaders that we elect to protect American independence.

In order to fix the problem; we must gain the legislative power to accomplish our goal of re-establishing the freedom that our founders intended for us. We cannot afford to hand over our power to government rulers. We have slowly learned that this does not work. Our political ruling class is so far out of touch and thirsty for power that they are unable to make decisions on behalf of the taxpayers. Instead they bow down to the voting blocks that secure their election to office.

Independence and self-reliance are two frightening concepts. Both are a necessity in a free society. The same can be said about freedom. Self-government requires hard work, but just like a good workout in the gym a healthier life will result. Personal development can be painful but it is absolutely necessary in a free Republic. We have the formula for success – our Constitution -it is time to implement it once again.

Americans can "hope" for change as long as they want, but until we roll our sleeves up and put in the hard work it takes to rid ourselves of oppressive taxes and ruthless rulers, we are not going to get it.

If you put your confidence into elected leaders you will end up disillusioned. We do not need politicians; we need taxpaying American citizens to serve in government.

A governing body cannot guarantee the protection of our best interests. Have faith in yourself. Be prepared for a challenge. Liberty and independence are not free – they must be earned. Get up off your couch and fight for what you want. I want to keep more of my earnings because it is the result of my own effort. **Adherence to our Constitution is the political equivalent to an insurance policy on our liberty. America is in need of an insurance policy. Americans cannot purchase personal insurance on our freedom; that is something that we must do for ourselves – through political action.** We have the ability to secure our own "political" insurance policy by running and electing the right officials - people that will stop the spending. We do not need "leaders" who encourage us to spend our money for the sake of falsely boosting the economy to increase their poll numbers. We cannot breathe new life into an economy that is built on paper currency, continuously rising tax rates and failing banks? I am not an economist, but I know paper is worthless.

Paper dollars have no tangible value. The American Dollar is simply a piece if paper that represents a promise of secured value. Paper cash is not good economic insurance. Recently, many economists have explored the idea of restoring the country to the gold standard because it is a tangible object that has had value for thousands of years. All the economics talk aside, as Americans; we need to take out an insurance policy on our liberty and our freedom. So start to research the difference between freedom and dependence. Only one is a life worth living.

Each time we are subjected to a tax hike we should see the ACLU (American Civil Liberties Union) lawyers out on the street fighting for the civil liberties of the American Taxslaves. We have the right to keep what we earn.

Where are the rights-based activist lawyers hiding out when it comes to economic enslavement of the American people? Why do they refuse to fight for the rights of the Taxslaves? Taxpayers are the people in need now - not only the protected minority groups. Taxpayers in the private sector are the people who go out and break their backs to support the public government employee unions and their inflated retirement pensions. As well, the taxpayers provide economic support for social welfare program recipients, public schools, unemployment entitlement and many other tax consuming, government-mandated dependence programs.

Taxpayers have become the little-guy being bullied around the schoolyard. Where are the civil rights activists and ACLU lawyers when it comes time for our rights to be protected? As taxpayers, we cannot afford lawyers to fight the government at the same time we try to earn enough to raise our families and pay our own bills. The government has an endless supply of financial and legal resources that "We the Taxslaves" provide through forced economic servitude.

Government uses our money to fight against us.

We actually fund the fight against ourselves!

This is insane; it is equal to self-imposed economic suicide.

Live the life that you preach to others – that is my message to the ACLU and other rights based activist groups. Stand and fight with us. Work to protect the American Taxslaves because we are suffering now. Big Government, Big Unions and wasteful social programs are draining our financial resources.

Join the fight or be ready for one.

Our leaders are not protecting us - they are enslaving us

Political bribery and economic extortion define our times.

Only you can release yourself from political captivity. Our situation will change when you turn yourself into a weapon of liberty. **Shepherds of deception are ruling American Taxslaves like sheep. We are subjects to an intellectual ruling class that has economically enslaved its subjects through the forced economic servitude of oppressive taxation.** Our government is spending at a reckless rate. Taxpaying Americans are burdened with responsibility, not only for the demands of their own lives and families, but also the demands placed on them by government to provide for their "communities". It is one thing to contribute your part for needed services that produce a better society, but it is another thing to sacrifice yourself for the well being of others that you are not responsible for. That must be a personal choice – charity must not be a government mandate that is forced upon us. We have the ability to regain our independence from Big Brother Government. We simply have to change our mindset from thinking that we "can't" to knowing that we "can".

Government can be "refreshed" every few years. Our entire government, on all levels, can be changed, refreshed and replaced in a matter of a few short years. We can do this every election cycle. I am not suggesting a full overhaul, because there are some good people in government - look no further than Texas congressman Ron Paul. There is a lot of red tape and bureaucracy that must be wiped out. We must support new candidates - home grown talent - not career politicians. Communities must create and grow leaders from the ground up. Elected officials must serve with the best interests of the taxpayers in mind. Taxpayers must run for office. We do not need more greedy, power hungry politicians. Our country is infected with enough of these people.

American taxpayers do not need politically ambitious rulers who work to advance at any cost for the sake of power and control. These characteristics mixed with an over inflated sense of self-importance are a poisonous recipe that can lead to a horrible result. We must elect regular individuals that earn a living in the free market - not from the pockets of taxpayers. America is in desperate need of people that actually want to sacrifice their time and energy to perform true public service.

Our duty is to find men and women who are ready to govern under the consent of the taxpaying portion of society. This is the only way to serve the best interests of the American people. True leaders will serve with honesty and integrity. Rulers will do what is easy. Leaders will do what is right.

Our elected "leaders" in local, state and federal office fail to realize the fact that high taxes are crippling taxpayers. As a result, they do nothing to effectively combat the threat to "We the Taxslaves". Property taxes are crippling homeowners, families, communities and our economy.

Oppressive taxes are crippling our cities and turning us into economically enslaved Tax Peasants.

We have become subjects; living under the rule of Tax Tyrants.

Rise of the Taxslaves

America has indeed ordered a cup if TEA. It is important for people to understand that the TEA Party is a reactionary movement. The future course of the TEA party will be dictated by what governments do in the future. If the spending does not come to an end, the TEA Party will only grow bigger and stronger. Look at what TEA stands for - **Taxed Enough Already**. So, it is no coincidence that most of the TEA Parties happen on or around April 15th - Tax Day.

TEA Parties are held to protest the forcibly imposed economic enslavement caused by the high taxes levied on taxpayers by Big Government. TEA Party members understand that we have become Tax Peasants. Both the Republicans and Democrats are to blame for this. **Both parties have merged into one national party - The Party of Big Spending.** Other than an "R" or a "D" by their names, both parties are essentially the same - two different heads that belong to the same beast - Big Government. Our society is splitting up into two divisions: Taxpayers and Tax consumers. The biggest disconnect is not between the Republicans and Democrats - the biggest disconnect is between the elected political ruling class and the taxpaying people.

The best thing about the TEA Party is that there is no single leader who we are rallying around. It is truly a movement "Of the people, by the people and for the people". TEA Party protestors are fighting for something bigger than control of a political party; we are fighting to keep more of what we earn and live free from forced economic servitude.

We want to change the current oppressive tax structure that allows government on all levels to legally confiscate our earnings. The TEA Party movements had a lot to do with the conservative victories in Westchester County, Virginia, New Jersey and Massachusetts. Politicians have been warned - serve the best interests of the taxpayers or else. Party affiliation will not matter; this is a true people's movement.

Undoubtedly, the major political parties will try to infiltrate and capitalize on the TEA Party movement to ride the wave to election into office, but I think people are waking up and will not be fooled. This will remain an independent movement of people that just want to be left alone. We want to take off the economic shackles and restore local power so that we can be in control of our own economic future. The next few elections will usher in the Rise of the Taxslaves.

This is a movement towards true conservatism, not the Republican Party. The TEA Party is made up of people that want more control of their own lives. Limited and responsible government is the ultimate goal. This is a revolutionary movement towards reclaiming our independence. TEA parties are individual revolutions that will change the politics of our country. This is not someone else's country, or someone else's government. Do not act like it is theirs - this country belongs to us –the American people who want to work hard for a better existence. This movement is ours - so force your government representatives to serve their intended purpose - to protect our freedom and let us live as free and independent men and women.

I have some great advice for our government– cut taxes and give the private sector an opportunity to prosper. History proves that this will lead to job creation, higher salaries, and higher pay for part time employees. Increased revenue for business leads to a more productive economy. Tax cuts will produce more tax dollars for government to spend on minimal, necessary services that "We the People" designate government to provide.

Government officials have wasted hundreds of billions of dollars in an attempt to forcibly turn our failing economy around. Politicians are doing everything except for what they need to do - **get out of our way.** Our rulers are doing this because they want to control things. If it works they get to take credit for "saving" us so that they can get re-elected and stay in power. If they fail, they can blame it on Capitalism and the "evil" free market. Unfortunately for taxpaying Americans, the temptation of gaining more power is much too tempting for our elected leaders to say, "No, you are not too big to fail".

Many business leaders are terrified of doing business in America. We have an economy that corporations are afraid of. Executives are unable to accurately forecast and predict a long-term business climate. They cannot accurately gauge what will happen a few years down the line. As a result, they are unable to project a realistic rate of expansion for sustainability. Most companies are unable to grow and expand because of our corporate tax penalties, suffocating tax code and volatile tax rates. Big Government and the political process have once again skewed the economic playing field.

Only "We the Taxslaves" can stop politicians from terrifying individuals and business owners with tax hikes, expensive healthcare mandates, and multi-billion dollar social programs that consume more and more of our earnings.

Government cannot force the free market to hire people unless they create more rules and regulations- this leads to higher prices on goods and services. There is a simple solution to the problem. By lowering the tax burden on corporations that do business here in the United States, the production and operating costs will be reduced, and therefore lead to a price drop in goods and services. Some politicians will say, "No, the greedy corporations will simply pocket higher profits". This can possibly happen, but those companies will quickly learn that competition drives prices down and will be forced to lower prices to stay competitive in a truly "free" market. The American people will benefit substantially from lowering tax on business here at home - this is a fact.

Government regulation and high corporate tax rates create a hostile environment for business operation. This degrades our economy. High taxes and government interference only make our lives worse.

I recently attended a city hall meeting in my hometown- the beautiful city of New Rochelle, New York. Our city manager mentioned that the city employees, on average have a salary package with benefits worth approximately $100k per year. That irritated me-because the average non-government employee's household income in New Rochelle is only about $50k per year. This means government employees earned twice as much as residents that make a living in the free market. There is something inherently wrong with that. Our city and school taxes are constantly raised from the current, hardly affordable existing tax rate. New Rochelle is in Westchester County. Here we have redundant services at our county level, which is the highest taxed county in the entire nation for the past three years in a row. Homeowners are forced to pay for overlapping, redundant services in our cities and villages. Simply put, we are paying for an unbelievable amount of waste. Because of redundant services (that can easily be cut) taxpayers are squeezed to the point that they are losing their homes. Our local leaders tell us that there is nothing they can do about it. They blame it on "union contracts" and "state mandates". Maybe it is time to go to war with the public employee unions. As well, I think it is also time for local governments to do battle with state representatives. **With the right people in office, it will not be that difficult to change our state of economic and political affairs.**

Our political ruling class has decided that they will be in charge of us. Their actions prove that they want to control all aspects of our lives. The housing market crashed in 2008 because liberal Democrats pressured banks to give loans that allowed high risk borrowers get into homes that they knew would be unaffordable. The reason why?

Votes.

Because of this, our ruling class has caused terrible damage to the American economy. They have done nothing to create real jobs – only public sector "government" jobs. **Our own government acts as a barrier to economic growth.** If they want jumpstart the economy and encourage job growth in the private sector (not government jobs) they must cut the tax rate. Companies generate more revenue when they keep more of what they earn, if taxpayers keep more of their earnings we would spend more. The free market works. As taxpayers we are barely able to withstand the economic assault imposed by our rulers. Lower tax rates will ensure that people will have more money in their pockets. When business owners apply less of their earnings towards taxes, they will put the money into product development, advertising, resource upgrades and new employees. Existing workers will even see pay increases. This is how wealth is created. Most good economists will tell you that cutting taxes creates wealth. History has proved this as well. Instead, taxes are constantly on the rise in order to support public employees and social program dependents. For example, most government employees on any level - local or national - have employment contracts and guaranteed yearly raises that are based on "time served" - not performance. So, essentially we are provided with the same level of service, but as taxpayers, we are paying more money for these services without an increase in efficiency or quality. The average American has been trained to believe that we "need" government employees to provide "necessary services". We are under the false illusion that the private sector cannot do it better or cheaper - we have been deceived.

It is unconstitutional for the Federal Government to treat one state different from another. Taxpayers in one state should not carry the burden of paying for services in another state outside of their own. How can we allow one person to pay for something out of pocket and then let another person get a government handout for the same service? One citizen pays for it while the other does not - this is not American!

Taxpayers must open their eyes and realize that we will not change this tax-madness until we put true public servants in office and remove the public serpents.

America needs people that are committed to shrinking the size of government and willing to cutting taxes. Because they have proven to be destructive, we need to run our elected officials not only out of office, but also out of town! **Any public official who fails to serve the best interests of taxpayers must be cast out of your community like a terrorist - a Tax Terrorist!**

Where has the character of our elected "leaders" gone? Character in government has disappeared because "We the People" lack the desire, mental aptitude, drive, and will power to hold our politicians and legislators accountable for the laws passed and the decisions made that have led to the demise of our economic security. **We have allowed our leaders to become rulers.** Too many Americans lack the integrity to fight for what is theirs - freedom, independence and their earnings. Why have we concealed our feelings of hostility when it comes to the political "games" when in fact, we need to release our emotions? Why continue our attempt to make honest men out of liars? We have become lazy and accepting. The American Taxslaves have no hope left.

Most Americans don't know who to listen to or who to believe? We no longer recognize honesty because it has been masked in so many lies. Despair and distrust have infiltrated our lives and we accept it. We must become uncomfortable with these feelings. Only when we become uncomfortable with the actions of our rulers will we be able to change our subservient behavior. We are being led down the wrong road.

Our rulers have successfully divided us - therefore putting "We the People" in a state of class warfare with each other. Our rulers are the enemy of freedom – not our neighbors.

Where is our President? Where is our Congress? Where is our Supreme Court? Why have they failed to work towards reducing the detrimental impact that poisonous legislation has made on our lives and our country? It is their job to protect us from all threats foreign and domestic. Abusive taxes are a threatening our freedom. We need protection from our own leaders. The people that have been elected to public office swear an oath protect our Constitution. They are not doing their job. Our elected "leaders" have failed to serve America.

Who poses the biggest threat to America? Is it the person with a bomb strapped to them? Is it the person hiding in a cave on the other side of the world? Or, perhaps the single greatest threat to America is the enemy within - the corrupt, power hungry politicians here in our own backyard that are incapable of effectively governing and doing what is right for the hard working Taxslaves of America.

As a result of the unsustainable rate of government spending, America is forced to borrow wealth from outside sources – like China. This destabilizes our economy and with it our domestic security. As more money is printed to satisfy this debt, we are faced with huge potential inflation that will surely destroy us and destroy any wealth or economic security that we work to build. American Taxslaves are staring into the eyes of a brutal economic collapse.

Foreign countries do not buy our debt because they think it is a good investment, they do it for political control. Foreign "investors" have the upper hand on us. They do it because they are investing in political capitol. Our "leaders" understand that we cannot simply print money because our currency will destabilize and lose value – and therefore hurt our economy and along with it the American people.

Despite this, the American Taxslaves are forced to pay higher taxes year after year. Although many homeowners are unable to pay their mortgages, they continue to give a bigger portion of their earnings to Uncle Sam – he gets his first. All we want to do is survive comfortably without government interference. Most Americans do not want to pay for the food, housing and healthcare needs of their neighbors. Our elected "leaders" have no form of economic balance. **Government-imposed Tax Slavery is destructive to the American way of life.** High taxes destroy families, homes, businesses and communities. Abusively high taxes destroy our hope for a better future.

We are fighting for one reason - to re-establish a Constitutional Republic and we are not willing to negotiate.

"We the People" are rising up, standing together; ready to take back control of our government. The American Taxslaves are rising and there is nothing that will put down our rebellion - and that is exactly what it is - a rebellion against a lawless political ruling class.

A fox is guarding the hen house

Members of our political ruling class have become architects of deceit. As taxpayers we passively sit back and accept the lies that are spoon-fed to us by the clean cut, well spoken, charismatic preachers of political poison. Most politicians lie; so do not blindly trust what they say. Instead, concentrate on their actions. If their lips are moving then they are most likely lying to us. **Americans have sentenced themselves to Tax Slavery because of political indifference.**

Our rulers are like emperors who show no restraint when it comes to spending our hard earned money. Each dollar that government spends is a dollar that has been forcibly confiscated from someone else. This "someone else" is usually some hopeless Taxslave who is not willing to stand up and say, "Stop taking what I earn". Although I am a Taxslave, I am not hopeless; I am hopeful - you better be too.

How can all Americans expect to have the best of everything if we do not work as hard as we can in everything that we do? People have different levels of discipline and work ethics – some of us sacrifice more than others in an attempt to create opportunities for greater success. Some of us simply work harder than others at achieving our dreams. America is the only country in the world where people travel with the hope of realizing their optimal potential and turning their dreams into reality. Why? It is because America is the land of opportunity. Hard work is required in America. Success in not a "right", and prosperity is not guaranteed.

We cannot make sure that everyone will be economically equal unless we give up control to a centralized planning body or a dictator. People have different abilities and work as hard as they choose to. The result of our hard work and effort is not guaranteed. Equal pay and equal living conditions will only be a reality if we give up our individual liberties and live under a ruler as an oppressed people. Sorry, but that's not my slice of pie. I want to control the conditions in my own life.

People are not economically equal and never will be – unless America, "the world's last best hope" "fundamentally transforms" into a fallen empire. I refuse to let these United States become some lost republic that future generations read about in their history books like Ancient Rome. If Americans become seduced by a Socialist mentality, and we allow ourselves to become subjects to our ruling class, it will be our own fault - because the resources to self-govern effectively are available for all of us to embrace.

An American fall from grace will be remembered by history as the most disastrous tragedy in the history of the world.

Our system of self-government only guarantees individual citizens opportunity. It does not guarantee success. Our founders laid the foundation for future generations to build upon. We have become an example of mankind's ability to provide for his own needs. We must be proud of our American heritage.

In the free market and a free society you get what you work for. For better or worse, our actions set us on the course of success or failure - not our government. Prosperity is not guaranteed. We might work hard and still not get what we want or feel we deserve. But, keep trying and maintain a state of continuous enlightenment through personal development. Although life's challenges seem impossible at times, we still live better lives than emperors and kings of the past could have ever imagined living.

Politicians are forcing us to pay the price for their costly mistakes. We pay different levels of government to provide services that private business can provide at a cheaper cost. **In many areas of the country, government public employee unions have a stranglehold on the taxpaying homeowners.** Property taxes are a poisonous tool of economic torture used by politicians to fund government. The most dangerous of these tools is the state mandate. The term is defined as *"a command or authorization to act in a particular way on a public issue given by the electorate to its representative"*.

American citizens are subjected to (among others) Federal and State government mandates. A State mandate is when taxpayers (usually homeowners) are sentenced to pay taxes that fund services that a specific level of government requires them to pay. There are typically two forms of mandates - funded and un-funded. With un-funded mandates, a lower level governing body pays the cost (usually from a separate layer of government revenue – like Federal down to State). Un-funded mandates are equal to forced economic servitude because a higher layer of government forces the lower, subservient level, to fund a specific program or service. Regardless of the economic burden, the local area government (town, city or, county) must pay the price – and as a result raises taxes.

Regardless of what level of government "pays for it" it is ultimately the taxpayers that are left with the check at the dining table. This is a sentence of forced labor thrust upon us by a ruling class. A mandate is an attack on each one of us as taxpayers - an enslaving tool used by the political ruling class on its subjects.

Our locally elected officials need to tell the Federal Government "Shame on you if you want my constituents to pay more taxes even though they do not have the financial means to do it".

Government relies on taxpayers for it's funding. Our elected rulers pass the bill onto "We the People". We are treated like Taxslaves. **Simply stated, a government mandate is free pass to confiscate and spend the earned income of a working taxpayer. It is a forced sentence of economic servitude that is a threat to all Americans.** Mandates pose a severe danger to our economic stability. Our rulers are slowly but surely working to break the spirit of the American people. Government spending results in continuous tax increases. This is a threat to us as individuals, business owners, and property owners. Even if you do not own a home and are working to save for one, the tax bill is coming out of your pocket because your landlord passes it to you. This increases the amount of time it will take for you to buy a home of your own.

Reckless government spending is wrong because it crippling the Americans taxpayers. Big Government interference must be put to an end. We can do this with our vote.

It is time for a rebirth of personal responsibility is America.

Taxation cannot bring prosperity to our country and our communities. Government cannot tax working people, and then spend to increase prosperity. There are no magical powers that will turn this approach from destructive to productive. When government on any level confiscates money from business it only hurts the free market economy. They are taking money from those who earned it. This "wealth" would otherwise be spent on goods and services created by the free market. Free flowing cash drives our economy into a feeding frenzy of economic prosperity. When consumers purchase goods and services government collects more revenue. Business transactions and job creation generate more revenue from sales tax on goods and from income tax on new jobs that are created.

Revenue generating businesses are being taxed out of their ability to hire new employees. As a result, many talented men and women are unable to start new and potentially promising careers. It is very difficult for working Americans to spend money on goods, services and long-term investments (like a home or business) when they are taxed at such an excessive rate. How can we be expected to spend what we do not have? We are already over leveraged. Because of this, politicians must stop spending and cut taxes on businesses and individuals - especially homeowners.

American taxpayers must fight to keep more of their earned income. If we are "allowed" to keep more of our earnings we will have more disposable income. As a result, we will spend. Because Americans love to spend, our economy will thrive and America will once again prosper therefore resulting in higher levels of employment. Jobs will be created when taxes are cut.

Our government has over spent itself. It is insane to think that the taxpayers can sustain the current level of taxation. **High tax rates are the equivalent to economic abuse at the hands of an out of touch ruling class.** Americans have become Taxslaves. We must break free from the Tax Slavery that is being forcibly imposed on us. Americans must fight back by electing people who have common sense into local and national office. Find candidates that are going to represent the values of hard working taxpayers. If you cannot find worthy candidates then you will need to develop them. Find leaders that can and will serve with integrity. If business owners can train employees to maximize profits and doctors can teach patients how to live healthy lives then why can't we train good people in our communities to serve the public interest and become honest politicians? The only way to achieve this goal is to remove the benefits and perks that are seducing people in public office.

America needs to elect regular men and women to office and fix the mess that our ruling class has created. This will not happen in one election cycle, but "We the People" need to start somewhere. Why not now?

We must break the economic barrier that exists between taxpayers and tax consumers - but first we must break the barrier between the rulers and the American people.

We have the ability to refresh our government every few years.

We have the ability to remove politicians who fail to serve the best interests of the American Taxslaves. We are fully capable of achieving this goal in a relatively short period if we all work together - towards our common goal of re-establishing the spirit of American self-reliance.

Our current politicians act as instruments of destruction. Honest public servants will save our republic. Because our leaders have power over our pockets, taxpaying Americans only stand to lose more and more if immediate political action is not taken. With each new government program or initiative "We the People" lose a bigger portion of our earned income. Working Americans are subjected to an uneven balance of government imposed financial obligation that exists between taxpayers and tax consumers. Our politicians are spending money like it grows on trees.

The American dollar is plummeting in both value and purchasing power. As we spiral further into debt, our money is worth less and less. Combine this with the fact that we keep less of what we earn and we get less for the prices that we pay. Who loses? The taxpayers lose despite the fact that we get up each day, go to work and pay our bills in a desperate attempt to meet our responsibilities and simply earn a living. We need to re-introduce ourselves to the "merit system" and condemn the "bailout system".

We have become a society of Taxslaves and government dependents. Too many of Americans depend on handouts even though they are fully capable of earning their own way. What is more degrading - being "taken care of" by your government when you do not need it - or working a job that you are embarrassed to have - like flipping burgers at McDonalds?

If you fall into the second category then you need to wake up. Look at the reality of your situation. Too many Americans are fully capable of working a productive job - but still accept unemployment because they feel "above" that kind of work. **It amazes me that someone fully capable of going to work will accept a government check and live day to day on**

unemployment when they do not really need to - knowing full well that they can physically get up and go to work. It may not be in the same field of work they had prior to being unemployed, but they can work to bridge the gap between employment opportunities. Most people still choose not to work a humbling job because they feel "above it" and feel entitled to something more. This is a problem that we must work to fix. **If we fail to take corrective actions, our society will collapse under the heavy burden of mass laziness and will be in deep trouble.**

Big Government is crippling taxpayers. The line has been crossed and the political elite ruling class makes no secret about their political plans. Tax and spend has become the trend of our time. This is not a secret - look at your paycheck or your property tax bill or your school tax bill. This is political thievery in action. As well, take a look at the sales tax that is forcibly imposed on almost every purchase that you make. Carefully observe every tax that is forcibly imposed on you - direct and indirect. Big Government has crossed the political and economic lines and overstepped the acceptable threshold of economic interference. It is now time for taxpayers to push government back to where it belongs. Taxpaying Americans cannot allow governments to dig further into our pockets.

Our political class is stealing our economic security and as a result doing great damage to our future. The time has come to take back what is ours – our hard earned economic property. The American Taxslaves must start to exercise their political authority. We must starve the beast of government and hit them where we will cause the most damage. We must cut the fuel off from the source – our wallets. If we sit by and fail to act, Democratic Socialism will be here before we know it. We cannot afford to lose our Republic; and along with it our liberty. Every dollar that our government commits to spend is making taxpayers worse off. There is no debating this. Government does not create jobs. It can only ease regulations and cut taxes. The free market will respond accordingly and as a result America will once again prosper.

How does a government create a job? Do they do it by hiring more government employees? This only wastes more taxpayer money and enslaves us further because "We the People" pay for their salary, benefits and pensions.

Government jobs cost taxpayers money because, after all, our tax dollars pay their salaries. The solution to economic turmoil is simple – **Tax Cuts.** Lowering the tax burden on Americans frees us up to spend more money-

therefore allowing more free market job creation from the resulting business growth. Let people keep more of what they earn and allow businesses have more money on reserve for product development.

By allowing business owners to gain a clear picture of their economic future, they will be more equipped to make more efficient short and long term planning decisions. Businesses assess their operational costs, and then make hiring decisions based on the results. More money equals more jobs and more production - this leads to more consumer consumption, which is the driving force behind any economy. Lower tax rates will allow businesses put more money into developing better products and therefore create more jobs. This is not rocket science; it is common economic sense.

Cripplingly high taxes are destroying the economic foundation of our nation. **Tax enslavement is shaking the foundation of our cities more violently than any bomb that has ever been deployed.** What is wrong with our political ruling class? What are they missing? We cannot attempt to fix politicians; we must get them out of office and fix ourselves. We can do this by putting honest, taxpayer friendly, constitutionally minded people into office. Reduced spending and tax cuts are necessary - this must be our ultimate goal. Americans must elect true patriots who will serve the interests of the taxpayers not - the public employee unions and other tax consumers who live off of the Taxslaves.

It is time to send a strong message to our elected officials - serve the interests of the taxpayers first - not the tax consumers. Go out to the voting booths and chop the unworthy politicians down like trees - your axe is your vote. We need tax cuts...and more tax cuts. Government employees and politicians must begin to show loyalty to the taxpayers who ultimately pay their salaries, benefits and retirement pensions. **Tax consumers living in strategically engineered voting districts are always going to vote for the person who will support "someone else" paying their bills.** Yes, I said it. These things need to be said. There are millions of other taxpaying Americans that feel the same as I do.

We will have our day in court. The trial of the century will be held on Election Day. Come hell or high water, we will bring freedom back to our lives and accountability back to our government.

Taxpayers are not stupid. We understand math. We look at the amount of money we have coming in to our households, then subtract our bills and expenses. This gives us a clear view of our financial status. If we spend more than we make, we are in trouble because we will be in debt. Working people understand this simple idea - unfortunately our politicians do not. Government is spending our tax dollars at a rate that exceeds their ability to confiscate it from us. Essentially, politicians are "spending" more than they are "making"- therefore creating public "debt". When this happens, politicians have two options to get out of debt. The first option is to raise taxes, which translate into taxpayers keeping less of their earnings. The other option is to print more money. These options are not available to taxpayers, only government.

A taxpayer in debt only has the option to work more and spend less. This is called sacrifice; and it is something that government can learn from taxpayers.

Do not allow yourself to be fooled when politicians "take responsibility" for over-spending. Regardless, the bills must be paid. Who pays for it in the end? The Taxslaves pay for it. If you recklessly drive down the street and kill someone with your car, is it enough to tell the grieving family "its ok, I take responsibility for this tragedy"? No!

There is a price to pay for reckless behavior. It is easy to be reckless when someone else has to deal with the consequences. It is easy to spend recklessly when someone else is paying the bill. So, the question must be asked; what are our elected officials going to do to fix the economic problems that their reckless actions have caused?

It seems as if our political ruling class thinks that they can fix our economic problems by spending more money. This is the same reckless behavior that got us into so much trouble in the first place. Politicians have spent, and have committed to spending way too much money.

The American Taxslaves are sitting on a mountain of debt. It is not acceptable for a man like the President of the United States to tell us that we have to spend our way out of an economic disaster? Look up the meaning of the word insane - it means doing the same thing over and over again each time expecting a different result. This is why I say that taxpayers have become victims of self-imposed stupidity. We keep electing people that promise to do the same impossible things - like cut taxes and simultaneously provide more government services. In reality, all they do is spend more of our money. I think we are crazy because we keep electing the same people over and over again while expecting a different result each time. American taxpayers are in for a rude awakening. Real change can only come when politicians stop spending our hard earned tax dollars. We must hold our politicians accountable for both their actions and their lack of action.

Our duty as Americans is to find the right people and to put them into public office. Too many of us are seduced by politicians because we feel a connection and think to ourselves "wow, he understands because he is just like me". News flash… they are not like us. Recall the words "Of the people, by the people and for the people". We need to elect men and women who have no desire to be life long politicians. We cannot restore accountability in government by electing leaders who want to live among the elite political ruling class.

As American citizens, we have the power to change the course of our political and economic future. This will only be possible when we begin to govern our own actions effectively. Only then will our elected officials realize that they cannot control us forever. Both Democrats and Republicans must get beyond the past political disagreements and move forward. Regardless of political party affiliation we must reduce the impact that government has on our wallets. Taxpaying Americans must ease the burden that the government has forced us to carry.

Politicians only listen to what we say leading up to Election Day; then it is back to business as usual for them and all integrity goes right out of the nearest window. This is the reason why we need to elect real people, not politicians, to serve in public office.

We must persistently battle against wealth re-distribution in any form. It is time to apply common sense to government spending. Our demands must be made very clear - government spending must be drastically reduced.

Government should only spend what is absolutely necessary and only on what is within its power to spend. The rules are outlined in our Constitution. Taxpayers must demand the truth when it comes to the allocation of influential political money that is "granted" to selected states and districts in order to earn politicians votes.

Our political process has turned into a cash grab. There has been a huge depreciation of accountability in both political parties because, regardless of party affiliation, our political rulers legally extort the income of hard working taxpayers.

It is time to remove the deceitful influence of government from our lives. American Taxslaves must initiate a revolution of the American Taxslaves.

The goal must be to reduce the size and cost of government. Americans have become an oppressed people who need to liberate themselves from an economically oppressive ruling class.

We live under tax tyranny in our own country. Our Republic has been taken over economically, financially and politically. Our ruling class has provided us with a steady supply of distractions ranging from celebrity scandals to mind-killing video games. We are being enslaved with out a single bullet being fired because we are living in a state of delusion. We must restore our sanity and fight for our economic independence from the Tax Tyrants of Big Government. Our indifference to the political process will be the weak point that leads to the fall of our freedom and independence.

There are two primary methods used to generate taxes the correct way. One is to build the tax base by encouraging people (and businesses) to move into a city or area. More residents living within a city will generate more tax revenue for the local government-therefore reducing the burden placed on property owners. The second way to generate additional "income" for government is to invite business into our communities by lowering taxes on the cost of operation. Remember, businesses generate tax revenue for governments and this helps ease the financial burden on taxpayers in the community. Local governments must develop creative ways to find some kind of inviting initiative to allow companies to move into American towns that have heavy tax burdens. Tax increases on homeowners and businesses will eventually cause them to leave town - and as a result decrease the tax revenue of our communities.

This is detrimental to American cities because it leads to a decrease in the tax base - therefore creating big problems for the residents who stay.

Over and over again we have seen once prosperous communities turn into poverty-afflicted ghost towns. Taxpayers who stay in these diminishing towns are forced to do more with less. Now it is time for government to do more with less. Our elected leaders must work hard to encourage businesses and encourage residents to build prosperous communities.

We are subjected to politicians and legislators who work hard to confiscate more and more of our earned income. It is our duty to protect our economic independence and uphold our commitment to liberty. We need to be modern day minutemen, ready at the drop of a hat – to go to war with our state and Federal Government officials. We must fight against the threat if Big Government. It makes no difference if you go to battle with your city, state or Federal Governments. If you want real change it is your duty to wreak havoc on your elected and appointed representatives. Do not be afraid to stand up and tell them "Enough is enough"! Reach out to your neighbors, friends, and families. Americans must win the war being waged against proven political ideas. We will do it if we focus on the two cornerstones of freedom- individual responsibility and economic freedom. This is our Republic, not theirs.

The Trial of the Century will be held on Election Day

It is time to liberate the American Taxslaves. Politically forced economic enslavement cannot continue. We must put our government on trial. Let the taxpayers be the judge and jury. We can provide the real facts and expose their actions. Let's have a public jury of real taxpayers decide just how guilty our officials are of forcibly imposed Tax Terrorism. America belongs to us, not them! Remember this - "We the People" means "We the People"- not "We the Rulers".

The TEA Party movement is an uprising of middle class homeowners and taxpayers who are fed up with the current economic enslavement that damages our personal and professional lives. As I stated earlier, the American people have been asleep. We have failed to pay attention to the political climate. **Unfortunately for those who gain from our oppression, we are slowly waking up.** In order to win the Political Super Bowl, taxpayers must learn the sport, understand the rules, and develop their own game plan for success. The TEA party people are not "stupid racist rednecks". We are the real American patriots who are intelligent, independent minded men and women who want Big Government oppression to be abolished. TEA Party participants are working to achieve freedom from Tax Tyranny and a restoration of limited and accountable government. We want to restore the foundation of freedom that America once represented.

The fuel for American achievement is individual responsibility, personal accountability, true public service, and self-sacrificing leadership.

The TEA Party uprising is a good thing. I cannot understand why TEA Party rallies were demonized in the media. Speaker of the House, Nancy Pelosi stood in front of a bunch of news cameras and cried "alligator" tears as she expressed her "concern" for the "hatred and violence" she allegedly witnessed. I have been lucky enough to speak at numerous TEA Party rallies that have totaled over ten thousand patriotic Americans since the movement started in the early 2009. Never once did I see hatred or violence. What I witnessed was the exact opposite; crowds of people who were filled with positive energy and a love for American independence. I was so happy to look around and see other people who felt the same way that I did. I witnessed a rebirth of American Patriotism. We are ready to stand up and peacefully fight the bully of Big Government.

At each rally, as I looked out into the sea of people I was treated to nothing but positive, uplifted and united American Taxslaves who came out to support a common cause of "We the People".

We want to remove the officials in office that are in favor of taking too much of what we work for. Do not be fooled by career politicians like Nancy Pelosi and the other actors of Political Theater who are strategically working to push their agendas. The Liberal goal of bigger government and greater control over the American people is being achieved through deceptive legislation that is detrimental to the economic sovereignty of hard working Americans.

Our ruling class has been successful up to this point because America is asleep. Times are changing and an uprising of American Taxslaves is underway. **The TEA parties are only the warning shots.** Just wait until Election Day. Americans will make a statement to both Republicans and Democrats; **Fight with us, or get out of the way.**

I am increasingly concerned about the harmful impact high taxes have on my life. I am anxious, and I am sure that many millions of American taxpayers are anxious as well. It is hard to imagine a better illustration of the tyrannical recklessness that is forcing us as taxpayers to do more with less while our government refuses to do adopt the same sacrificial approach to spending. American taxpayers are on the brink of total government control of the economy. I work in Manhattan; so every campaign season

I see tons and tons of campaign materials, stickers and signs on every street corner. A few years ago, I noticed a campaign sign that caught my attention for all the wrong reasons. The sign read:

"Francis Villar for mayor of New York. Tenant organizer student activist, working mother, and socialist. Challenge the billionaires. Put poor and working people first...vote for socialism and liberation".

Put poor and working people first? What about putting taxpayers first? What about the people who go out and earn their own living? When did this become acceptable? We must tell all Socialists to "Love it or Leave it". If you want Socialism you should move to Europe and resurrect the USSR - good luck and good riddance!

This is America - "home of the brave", it must not be "home of the Taxslave". We must increase our opposition to Big Government. We have not focused close attention on the actions of our "political rulers" and as a result we have slipped into a state of government control. Little by little the American Taxslaves are waking up- like little flowers blooming under the sunshine of freedom.

If we each tend to our own "political gardens", pretty soon things will be beautiful again. The left leaning ice age of Big Government will come to an end.

True conservatism is in full bloom. Americans are calling for restoration of limited government. The spending habits of our political ruling classes represent a clear and present danger to American economic freedom. If we do nothing, our freedom will disappear. Taxpayers must rise to the challenge and restore sanity to this land of political confusion.

Our leaders earn the harsh criticism that they get. Taxpaying American citizens also deserve their fair share of criticism for doing nothing to combat the forced economic servitude that we have come to accept.

Town hall meetings are where the battle-lines will be drawn. State your demands, call for political action and put in the necessary work to educate your friends and neighbors.

It is a lot more difficult than we think it is to find something of consistency. Currently, we have a fifty-fifty shot at staying married in this country. Our desires seem to change overnight. It is very difficult to find something or someone that sticks to their commitments. We need to find people that are reliable to run for office - men and women that will keep their word and stick to their commitments. We need to put true public servants in office; men and women who will show loyalty to the taxpayers and effectively serve our Constitution as it was intended to be served. **The economic welfare of the taxpaying portion of society must be made a priority. A loyal commitment to limited local, state and Federal Governments must be a priority of anyone that is elected to serve in public office.**

Electing committed men and women to serve in government will only be the first phase. The second phase will be achieving the passage of legislation that will restore sanity to government spending, reduce dependence on government for employment, retirement, and entitlement programs.

It is time for "Big Brother" to grow up and get out of our house

This may sound harsh, but we must make the difficult decision to get government out of every aspect of our economic lives. A family cannot be strong and prosperous unless it takes care of its own needs first - then and only then will the majority of Americans take part in charitable acts on a more frequent basis. We must work hard to provide economic safety, stability and security for ourselves. Once we achieve this, we can then work towards providing help for others. **Charity and forced economic servitude are not the same things. Charity comes from a place of good intentions designed to help those who are truly in need of temporary assistance. Taxation in the form of wealth re-distribution is more aligned with forced economic servitude and Despotism.**

Cars, computers, Ipods, and other produced goods are quality products, but they are made relatively cheap. They have short shelf lives, most are not durable, reliable and maintenance free. This applies to politicians as well, since they do not always mean what they say and say what they mean - in other words, they are not reliable **political products**. We are often tricked into thinking that we have a political candidate of quality and substance when in reality it is all advertising and nice packaging. Most of us understand that it is essential to do our research before we make a big financial investment in something. **It amazes me to see how little research most of us put into our political investments. We invest in politics** when we cast our vote for particular candidates. Take a moment to honestly reflect on how you've spent your political capital.

We are never more than a few bad political decisions away from ending up in another Nazi Germany or Stalinist Russia.

Most bad political investments come from a poor understanding of the impact that our votes will have on our lives. Have you ever voted for a candidate that turns out to be of a lower quality than expected? **When it comes to bad politicians, we cannot return them, but we can make the decision to never "buy" that "product" again.**

Politicians spend too much of our money and place a massive burden on the taxpayers of America. They are examples of "political" products that do not operate as advertised. Therefore we must work to achieve change. I do not mean change for the sake of change, rather, real change for the right reasons. Americans need a political class that will make the right decisions even if the choices are difficult to make. Our elected officials must do what is right for the taxpayers. The American Taxslaves must lead the way to greater personal responsibility.

Only when we assume responsibility for our own actions we will be able to guide those who do not have the ability to assume personal responsibility in their own lives.

Americans are in desperate need of leaders who encourage people to earn a living on their own. All Americans are capable of living fulfilled and rewarding lives. Tomorrow can be better than today if we put in the necessary work to improve our lives and assume personal responsibility for our own lives today. The feeling of independence gives birth to true freedom - and freedom is in our best interests. We will only achieve our potential when we become free from economic oppression and financial dependence on government. Once when we work to reach the height of our own ability will we be able to lead others towards the same achievement. There are people who, when there is one slice of pizza left, will say "I'll split it with you". But, there are others who will say, "you can have the last slice, I'll find something else to eat". I am the kind of person that will find something else to eat. I do this by choice. Americans are caring, generous and compassionate people. But, unless we can stand on our own stable economic ground first, we cannot help each other. Handouts only degrade the character and resolve of our nation. We must work to get ourselves balanced on stable financial ground before we can help build up those who are not stable.

Economic enslavement cannot be tolerated. Dependence on government for your survival must not be an option. Economic enslavement is destructive. Tax Slavery is destructive to the soul of America. Tax Tyrants are stealing the future of these United States. Government has become a gang of political and economic bullies. City hall and other levels of government target the people who cannot fight back. They prey on the weak - like most of us "middleclass" Taxslaves, who are struggling to pay bills and live our lives free and independent of Big Government. Taxpayers, and especially property owners are in a position where we cannot afford to disobey the Tax Terrorists of government; they hit us where it hurts the most - in our pockets.

How many homeowners can afford their mortgages but not their inflated property taxes? I live in New York - Westchester County to be exact. We have the highest property taxes in the nation! If we cannot afford to pay the gross taxes on our homes –the government will confiscate our property. Like gangsters, they always collect. Instead of breaking our legs, they break our lives, our families and our economic backbone. If you cannot afford to pay your property taxes, your government will confiscate your home. This kind of legal extortion must come to a quick and abrupt end.

Out of control taxes are a threat to the American way of life. We have been stricken with an economic burden that no free American should tolerate. High taxes have consequences. What are the consequences? From a personal perspective it affects individuals. It takes money out of the pockets of Americans that would otherwise be used to provide better necessities for their own families. As well, high taxes take away from businesses and employment opportunities. Simply put, excessively high taxes hurt all of us. We need massive budget cuts across the spectrum of government. Local governments prepare budgets in order to provide necessary services to local residents. Homeowners also have necessary "services"; there is a hierarchy of needs in our communities. The taxpayers ultimately fund government, so it no secret that our needs should come first. We must establish a **Taxpayer Hierarchy of Needs.** We need to keep what we earn. We need to take care of our needs before the needs of others - unless we choose to be charitable. Charity is a choice. **Wealth redistribution is forced economic servitude.** It must be our choice to spend what we earn as we see fit. Ultimately, we need to rely on ourselves to meet our own needs.

America was intended to be a country governed by men within the limits of our Constitution. Unfortunately for us, we have become a country governed by rulers who work to satisfy their own needs. Elections, and as a result, politics have become a popularity contest. Elections are easily won by well-funded advertising campaigns that are backed by big industry, big unions and a ruthless political class of conspirators. Government like this is not in tune with what our founding fathers had in mind. This type of political poison shows contempt for a free body of people.

We are surrounded by Devils in Disguise

Our "leaders" ask us to follow as they lead us on a path towards freedom, independence, and prosperity. Unfortunately, their actions do not match their "good" intentions. They are indeed devils in disguise leading us down a path of forced servitude and oppression. Instead of keeping their promises, our rulers (who swear an oath to protect us) have led us into economic enslavement. Once we reached out and grabbed their hand for support, they put their shackles on us. Rather than lead us to liberty, they have dragged us towards political and financial enslavement.

It is clear to see that our ruling class is to the taxpayers what Judas was to Jesus- two-faced hypocrites who lack the honor and integrity to stand by their words of promise and loyalty. Our politicians do not stand by their commitments. They play party politics and use political bribery to achieve seats in public office. My message to them is this; your reign is coming to an end. It may not be this election or the next election, but rest assured the spark of liberty has ignited a small flame and it is slowly growing. Soon, the flame of political independence will consume the unworthy men and women who have led us down the path to economic servitude.

America was not founded on the idea of playing "follow the leader". As sovereigns we are individual kings – "We the People" are the true leaders of this nation. We are the soldiers in the war for freedom and independence from the enslaving taxes that are demanded by our ruling class. America must once again fight to secure freedom from oppression. Each of us must do our part to maintain American Independence. We are in the middle of a struggle to restore sanity back to our to government.

We must not lose ourselves in the political chaos that reign's supreme. If we do, we may never win back our freedom from tyrants. A huge challenge is ahead of us. This is our chance to write a new chapter in American history. We can show the world what it means to be American. Once again we have a chance to remind the world that a free and independent people can achieve greatness through self-governance.

In order to remove the filth that has become Big Government and its oppressive tax structure, Americans need to shed the skin of dependence and exfoliate the dead "political cells". American Taxslaves must evolve into political activists. It is critically important to understand that when it comes to politics, America has become an un-informed and un-involved country. This can be easily fixed. We must educate ourselves so that we can understand the strategies used against us. It is important to understand that a ruling class of comptemptous legislators has taken our power as individuals away from us and given it to Big Government.

Americans must gain an understanding of what our founder's intended when they wrote our Constitution. **It is our duty to isolate and identify those who trespass against our founding principles and understand that their weapon of choice is deception.** This will allow us to arm ourselves for the political and legislative battle ahead.

A despotic governing body once again threatens "We the People". Political inaction is equivalent to cowardice. Lack of action will only leave us enslaved by a ruling class. You cannot afford to sit back passively hoping to be saved. Freedom from a threatening adversary requires action. I hate to break the bad news, but our rulers will work relentlessly to keep us in a constant state of dependence. There is no flying under the radar if you are a taxpayer. Does the IRS ring a bell? If you protest government spending, by not paying your taxes, they will either throw you in jail or forcibly take what you have earned - including your home. American Taxpayers are in trouble. We cannot afford to sit back and do nothing.

Like a spoiled child, government gets what government wants.

American taxpayers should be treated like a preferred customer. Instead, the "pay your fair share" income tax structure is punishing financial success and prosperity. Taxpayers provide government with the funds it needs to operate - just like customers do for businesses. What happened to the idea of "The customer is always right"? It is been changed to " The government is always right".

We have been thrown off course because we are comfortable. As a result, change is badly needed. We must work to restore the idea that the best interests of the taxpayers must be served before those of the tax consumers. Americans must resurrect the merit system. Taxpayers must not allow more than a small percentage of their earnings to be confiscated. Free people are entitled to keep what their efforts earn - otherwise they cease to be free, and become Taxslaves.

The American Taxslaves are slowly waking up. Most of us are getting up on the wrong side of the bed and we are in a bad mood to say the least. I wake up every day ready to fight for what is mine. I want to keep more of what I earn. All American taxpayers must refuse to let the economic result of their hard work continue to be confiscated then redistributed as politicians see fit.

How are we "free" if government officials can raise our taxes, steal our earnings, fine us, confiscate our property and even throw us in jail?

My question to our rulers; "Who the hell do you think you are"? By birthright, I am a free man - my rights are "endowed by my Creator"- so leave me alone, and leave the American Taxslaves alone.

My government does not give me the right to live free - God does.

According to Natural Law and our Constitution, Governments are "instituted among men" to protect our freedoms.

"Governments are instituted among Men, deriving their just powers from the consent of the governed, — That whenever any Form of Government becomes destructive of these ends, it is the Right of the People to alter or to abolish it, and to institute new Government...."

Re-read that last part again-

"...whenever any Form of Government becomes destructive of these ends, it is the Right of the People to alter or to abolish it, and to institute new Government...."

Have we reached the point yet? Yes!

It is essential that we understand the fact that our government does not create rights. Rulers and dictators create rights. Big Government and ambitious power hungry politicians in Washington, as well our own city halls have created a political and economic crisis. We are tricked into believing that these men and women are in problem solving mode for the good of the American people. Politicians demand more money from taxpayers to "fix" the problems that <u>they</u> cause in the first place. My message to Big Government is this; "Leave us alone, you are the problem, so get off of our backs; we will be fine without you".

Americans must remember that this is our government and our country. Our Republic was earned through blood by a generation of patriots - so that our generation can maintain it with our votes.

Our political rulers are intoxicated with the arrogance of power. Our so-called "leaders" show blatant disregard for the American Taxslaves who have been reduced to peasants - struggling amid a severe economic downturn. From city-to-city, town-to-town, state-to-state and coast-to-coast taxpayers are being asked to pay more into government for unnecessary programs, and wasteful public services. Some public services are necessary to a limited degree, but the bill for government operation has become agonizing and painful. The free market can provide many of the same services that government currently provides at a much cheaper cost, in a more effective manner. If our movement is successful, the American Taxslaves will no longer have to finance the retirement pensions of tax consuming government employees.

Since government is looking out for its own interests, we as taxpayers must look out for ourselves. We must elect good and honorable candidates into seats of public office who will not be afraid to make the necessary changes that the members of our current ruling class refuse to make.

The American people have embraced the lies that both liberal and conservative politicians have served up. We have embraced the lie that it is the role of government to take care of its citizens. Politicians are incapable of giving us what we need. As unique individuals we are very different from one another. Our varying work ethics prove this. Hard work and risk taking will potentially lead to greater prosperity. Some of us work hard and take risks while others do not – so, how can we all have the same things? Remember this simple fact; whatever government gives out, it must first take from another American who has earned it. This is the equivalent to legal thievery and forced economic servitude.

Government officials should not be activists. Upon being sworn into office, our elected leaders swear an oath to protect the Constitution. They swear to protect us from all threats foreign and domestic. Nearly all of our elected officials have failed to live up to their end of the bargain. They have failed to protect the American Taxslaves from the political and economic extortion that is imposed by a political ruling class.

Politicians rack up countless votes simply by voting in favor of legislation that takes from one segment of society and redistributes it to another.

As free men and women we must earn our own way through life. Financial success should not be punished. Instead, economic prosperity should be viewed in a positive light - to motivate us towards achieving what is possible on our own. But, we must work hard for success of any kind - not only financial success, but in all aspects of our lives. A huge percentage of our earnings should not be confiscated and re-distributed due to the fact that some people have more than others - simply because they don't work as hard or implement the same level of discipline in their own lives. This is Anti-American and to say the least - unfair. The simple solution is to liberate the Taxslaves by implementing a more free tax system. After much research I have become a big fan of a flat, consumption based tax system. I suggest that you research this for yourselves. You will be very, very surprised and excited about the prospect of a new "Fair" tax system.

It is time to change the channel and tune into a new political frequency. Find the courage in your heart and the wisdom of mind to actively pursue liberation from government imposed Tax Slavery.

We have to begin dividing the responsibility paid in taxes for communities between individuals and government.

Government should be delegated to provide only the basic needs and services that American citizens choose not provide on their own.

Citizens delegate responsibility to their local, state and Federal Government for specific services. If the free market can provide these services at a better price - without long-term pension obligations, then it should be done. The problem is not with government provided services, but the quality and cost of these services – they are too expensive for the taxpayers to fund.

Government employees are paid much higher salaries than the average private sector employee - almost double! The average private sector employee earns a salary of approximately $40, 000.00 per year. Compare that to the average government employee's salary. The average pay per federal worker is roughly $75, 000.00. It is frustrating to most taxpayers to know that civil servants are paid nearly twice as much as the average American working in the free market. **Most taxpayers - myself included, would not mind government employees making a ton of money if they cut taxes significantly and kept spending and taxes under control.** If they saved us money in return, I would not mind paying higher wages - I would actually embrace them. Unfortunately, this is not the case.

Instead, taxpayers are treated like a blank check that is used to fund costly, *government-promoted* entitlement programs. These programs are used as tools of economic enslavement - to secure re-election for a ruthless political class of unworthy thieves who use political bribery to secure votes. As a result of this, the tax-consuming portion of society has become disconnected from the cost of government. The burden is placed on the back of the taxpayers. People who do not pay taxes demand that the "government" provide more services-for "free". This applies to the tax consuming public employees more than any other type of tax consumer. Public employees and entitlement recipients never feel the financial whiplash that results from the tax increases needed to meet their economic demands - because the Taxslaves ultimately pay their bills.

Economic enslavement through wealth re-distribution and blatant Tax Slavery are not characteristics of a free American society. The redistribution system of wealth is being imposed on the American Taxslaves. Because of this, we have become economically enslaved peasants to Big Government. This is accomplished by their manipulation of the voting of block of dependents that rely on government for "free" handouts or "guaranteed" employment. Our elected rulers have imposed terrible financial hardships on the taxpaying portion of American society.

The three branches of American government are no longer made up of leaders; they are made up of rulers.

I take the concept of "wealth redistribution" personally - we all should. As a result, we must work hard to combat the problem of Big Government mastery over the American citizens. You can do your part by speaking out. Fight at your local level of government. Work hard to keep government influence out of all aspects of your life. Free men do not need to be told what to do and how to do it. We must restore America back to a country ruled by laws - not politicians and campaign cash. From our movement, a new generation of founding fathers will emerge. We must swear commitment to positive political action at the local level.

Fear of serving a ruler must compel us to act.

If we fail to act now, even more of what we work for will be legally extorted by our government-only to be handed out to those who do not earn an honest days pay. I am afraid, but I am ready to fight. I know that I am not alone in my fear or my commitment to fight the necessary battle for my independence. Leaders will emerge and a new generation of American Revolutionaries will push back against Big Government.

Now is the time to show some backbone and stand defiant in the face of forced economic servitude. Point your finger in the face of Big Government and say, "Don't tread on us". This is the time to stand united. We cannot allow ourselves to be divided. Our time in American history will be a shining example of what refreshes American Independence. Our political ruling class is the newest form of tyranny. Our rulers continue to use various forms of media to paint a fabricated picture of a free America.

Do not be fooled, resist the un-natural desire to trust your government.

I have no idea what the future will bring, but I do know what America can bring to the future. Our generation can bring a restoration of limited government and personal responsibility. This new American Crisis can be resolved if we reduce our dependence on government to provide for our own needs. We must train ourselves to rely on nothing but our own abilities. I rely on my own abilities to provide for my own needs. I rely on myself – not my neighbors. I want the freedom to succeed and freedom to fail. I know that I will be fine if I am left alone to control the course of my own life.

Our cries for freedom have been ignored – so stop crying out for help and help yourself.

Anytime a person or group becomes dependent on someone else for his or her security and economic stability they become enslaved. At that point freedom is replaced by dependence - and dependence is the same as enslavement. Do not give up control of your own lives-stand up and fight. Do not bow-down to a master of any kind.

As an American, you are a sovereign; an individual king - so wear your crown of independence with pride and pass it on to the next generation! America cannot allow it's elected officials to live for today and sacrifice tomorrow. *America must be forever.*

We will win this battle by removing our elected rulers from office. The current political ruling class is not a good example of how a representative government should work. A Republic can only work when the people hold their elected officials responsible for their actions. We have an out-of-control government on all levels - from local to federal. We must impose constitutional limits on the actions of our political ruling class. Taxpayers have been left in the dark and stuck with the check. Government is like a person who orders the most expensive thing on the menu, eats it, and then leaves the bill for someone else to pay.

What do we do when we are left with a bill too big to pay? You roll up your sleeves and wash dishes. It is now time to wash the dirty dishes of Big Government.

The solution is simple - we cannot spend more money than we have. We are constantly "treated" to new legislation that is enacted to provide new services at an unaffordable cost to the taxpayers. Middle class Americans do not reap the benefits of the programs that cost them more tax dollars.

Do our elected "leaders" actually believe that spending more money will solve an economic crisis that is a direct result of government spending?

If this is true, then we must tell them - loud and clear - that they are too stupid to govern. It is visibly evident that Americans are faced with unsustainable debt, enslaving taxes and incapable legislators. Therefore, we must remove them from office, and replace them with honest and capable public servants who will listen when we tell them that continued spending is no longer an option.

Guard your independence jealously Protect it with ruthless passion

Big Government is the serpent that is tempting us to eat from the tree of political dependence. The road to success will be achieved by removing the political parasites that have degenerated American Independence. We cannot trust our elected officials, but we can trust our Constitution. It is fully within our ability to make sure that our "leaders" are doing what they were put in office to do - protect America from all threats – foreign and domestic. **We are watching President Obama attempt to "fundamentally transform" us from a free and independent people to an enslaved, dependent group of peasants.** The fate of our Republic is being sealed before our eyes. It is our responsibility to do our part to save our freedom, our Constitution and our Republic. We have the ability to restore individual freedom, liberty and independence. "We the People" must not allow ourselves to be enslaved by a despotic governing body.

Ariel Durant summed it up perfectly when he said,

"A great civilization is not conquered from without until it has destroyed itself from within".

Up to this point Americans taxpayers have argued with our political ruling class without success because we compromise too easily. We can no longer travel down this path. Simply stated, we must to get rid of our "ruling" class and replace them with a "serving" class. The American Taxslaves will achieve this at the voting booths. Our politicians have steered us so far left of center that this generation has come to expect governments on all levels to give us what we need to survive. This is not independence; it more closely resembles dependence. We must put new leaders in office who are willing to make responsible decisions and vote on policies that protect the best interests of the taxpaying portion of American society. **We can no longer allow ourselves to be held hostage by tax consuming government dependents and public employee unions who demand more and more of our earnings.**

Government provided services cost taxpayers time, effort and money - all which are valuable. So, when someone gets something for "free" from the government, another person ultimately has to pay for it. As I stated earlier, government has no wealth of its own, only what it "legally" confiscates from one to give to another. Government provided handouts and bailouts must be stopped. Each of us must learn to rely on ourselves to satisfy our own needs. We must shift our mindset from thinking government should do it for us, to knowing that we can do it for ourselves. We do not need assistance from a big, economically oppressive government – we need them to get out of our way.

"We the People" are the only thing that stands between freedom and enslavement. Fear of further economic enslavement has opened my eyes. Now, I am making an attempt to lead the way and guide others down the path towards enlightenment. Homeowners and taxpayers have a great deal to lose. Doing nothing is not an option. We must stop our legislators from sneaking through legislation at the last minute without even reading the contents. This has become accepted and expected – even though it is in direct opposition to our best interests as a free nation. It is a shame that this type of political behavior has become acceptable. We must stand up for liberty and fight against the rise of Big Government and the resulting economic tyranny.

Most Americans show a lack of interest in the political process. This has jeopardized both our freedom and our liberty. We must rescue ourselves from the disaster of Big Government. Our salvation will come from a restoration of limited, responsible government and true individual freedom. We must take control of our own lives and liberate ourselves from dependence on a ruling class. Citizens elect leaders to make decisions on their behalf, and, unfortunately, their power over our pockets is growing. Politicians have developed an addiction to spending what "We the Taxslaves" earn. Rather than develop real solutions to problems, they have become the problem. Many legislators and government officials work full-time to find ways to make the American people part with their hard earned income. This is not about money - it is about what we need to maintain our lives free from the fear of economic struggle. Many Americans are struggling to get by each day. Despite this, more and more is being asked of us each day. It is time to cancel the blank check and close the Bank of The Taxslaves. **If we are going to survive we will have to curb government's appetite for our tax dollars.** First, we need to curb our own appetites and become responsible for our own needs.

Individual responsibility, personal accountability, courage and freedom are all characteristics that have made America a great nation. It is too far into the American experiment to collapse under the pressure of self-government. We cannot cower down and accept things as they are just because we don't want to get involved in politics. Courage in the face of danger and a spirit of achievement is what made America what it is today. Revolution is good if it is waged against those who seek to oppress the minds of men. Political awareness combined with action is what will keep us free from tyranny. We need to get our elected officials on the same page as us so that we can put this creepy chapter of American history behind us. It is time to start a new chapter - one that restores limited, self-government under the "Consent of the governed".

In order fort this resurrection of America to take place, the "governed" must understand how our political system was intended to work - and, more importantly, understand that we have a responsibility to elect men and women who will protect freedom at any cost. We cannot allow politics to remain a popularity contest. Some people have no business voting in elections, because they do not understand what a Republic is. **The election process must not be used as a tool to negotiate the most out of what government can do for us.** American citizens must take the time to understand that liberty is easily lost. "We the People" are the only true protectors of our own fate. Infuse yourselves with knowledge - because reality will eventually shine through political deception.

When Americans rise up and fight against the newest form of economic tyranny, we will liberate ourselves from political enslavement. Cowards cannot preserve a free existence. Revolution will not require physical violence towards our ruling class. It simply requires that you openly speak your mind and work to change the current system of political malpractice that is "comfortably" in place. All Americans must work together in the pursuit of liberty. The most destitute among us - those who live off "the system", will become angry. They are the people who, in the long term, have the most to gain from the political "destruction" of our oppressive ruling class.

America is facing a crisis - the demise of Constitutional rule of law. We cannot allow our legislators to turn a blind eye to the Constitution. Legislators, judges and politicians are playing a political game at our expense. I know that I am not a free man- I am a Tax Slave. Why do members of our ruling class have the legislative authority to determine what percent of our "hard work" we will get to keep? These people must be held accountable for this form of legal extortion.

It is your duty to start paying attention to what is going in Washington, but more importantly, you must begin paying attention to your own City Hall. How many of us actually have real relationships with our local representatives? Our senators and congressmen have become celebrities to us - simply because we see them on television. They have become celebrities to themselves. Our rulers are out of touch. They are not reachable by the average citizen unless it is campaign season. Can the average non-politically active citizen get in the ear of their locally elected officials? The answer is no. I am willing to bet that if one million enthusiastic American Taxslaves plant themselves at the foot of the White House steps, our rulers will pay close attention. This is what will get us back on track.

American taxpayers have become pawns in a game that is being played by our rulers. The shame falls on us for allowing this to happen. We must become men and women who are in control of our own economic destiny. I will never apologize for vilifying politicians. Our rulers have damned themselves by their own treasonous actions. Their social programs are destructive to the taxpaying portion of society.

Our rulers have put themselves in a state of war with the American Taxslaves.

The American Republic is facing a real threat, and too few of us are paying attention. Taxpayers must take bold and decisive action to combat the threat of Big Government. We have become subjects to an unapologetic ruling class.

Our political "leaders" have created a false image of a free society – our freedom is an illusion. We are not living as free men. Yes we can come and go as we please to the store or on vacation and move around freely.

However, when it comes to the cornerstone of freedom - home ownership - we are on the hook for a boatload of money through enslaving property taxes.

Americans work, save and sacrifice to become homeowners. In the process massive debt is incurred by way of interest on mortgage loans and other associated costs. Once the "American Dream" of homeownership is realized we are forced to pay "rent" on our own property. Property tax is equivalent to rent on our own home. Property tax is the most oppressive form of taxation. The political ruling class has abandoned the American taxpayers. We have been left to fend for ourselves with the scraps that are left after they have taken their "fair" share. Taxpayers are hungry and do not want scraps. We do not need handouts - we simply need the **government-imposed extortion** to stop. American taxpayers want to be left alone - so that we can keep the majority of our earnings. We have the ability to take care of our families, our communities, and ourselves. Each of us must tend to our own needs.

Once we are financially secure, we will be charitable.

Unfortunately for the American taxpayers, we cannot get a divorce from Big Government. I believe that the time for separation us upon us.

It is time to divorce Big Government - they are already taking half, so what else do we have to lose?

Each one of us must work hard and prepare for a difficult fight so that we can enjoy the financial safety and economic security that will come.

We send terrorists to prison and the Tax Terrorists are sent to serve in political office. It is time to come to our senses. Politicians must not be allowed to conceal their intentions and sneak in legislation that is detrimental to taxpayers. It sickens me to know that members of our spineless political class rely on poll results to determine where they should stand on important issues. Unfortunately, we are so busy paying taxes that we are not paying attention. Let me simplify this for any politicians that might be reading this - Say what you believe, uphold your promises and let us decide if you are worthy of serving the best interests of "We the People".

Concealed intentions must be banned from politics. Our elected officials, along with taxpayers must work to reduce the cost of Big Government. The value of America is not only measured in dollars, but also more importantly, the value in weight of self-determination.

America has been the cornerstone of freedom and success. America is great because of what past generations have achieved in the face of great challenges. Americans have endured and fought past many complicated struggles.

Many Americans are under the false illusion that success is guaranteed. Sadly, success is not guaranteed, only the ability to try is certain. We always see movies and hear stories about the little guy who beat all of the odds and achieved impressive success (The movie "Rudy" still brings a tear to my eyes). We must keep in mind that for every success story there are plenty of unhappy endings. Life cannot and does not always play out like an Oscar winning movie. Despite this fact, we still strive to be the best that we can be. Lately our attitude has shifted to expect success instead of working for it. We want our needs fulfilled by government. We want things handed to us simply because we are American and because of that we think we deserve it. This mentality has created a generation of dependents that do not try hard enough to achieve realistic goals. This is disgraceful.

It is essential that all Americans work hard to restore the ideals of personal responsibility and accountability. These are the true foundation of freedom, liberty, and independence. **Too many of us have become "wanters" and "expecters". The majority of Americans are no longer dreamers and explorers.** Instead we demand that government hand things over to us simply because we exist. This is not the American way. The American dream is not guaranteed, only the opportunity to achieve it through sacrifice and hard work is.

If you are a tax consumer (social program recipient or government employee), remember that what you are "given" is being provided at the expense of someone else. Your hard working neighbors are paying for your "free ride - so stop expecting more and more. Taxpayers are "sacrificing" more and more of their earnings each year, so my message to tax consumers is this; leave the system of Big Government. Union protection will not protect you from your neighbors once they realize that you are the cause for their economic hardships. Public employee unions are hurting homeowners through the massive taxes needed to fund their sweetheart pensions and life-long benefits.

I have a warning for all tax consumers - because of you, our country is dying a little more each day, and as a result, you are becoming the fuel behind our revolution.

Be careful, the economic police are on the hunt for you. Government would rather forcibly confiscate more and more from taxpayers instead of setting an example by making necessary cuts. Revolution is indeed brewing. As a result of political recklessness, revolution is once again threatening the political class of these United States. This is the natural course of action. America is no longer a Representative Republic. We more closely resemble a monarchy. The American people have become subjects to a political ruling class that dictates what we get to keep and decides what is confiscated for redistribution.

It does not take a genius to govern – all it takes it takes an honest person.

We are left with one option - a Taxslaves Revolution

Thomas Jefferson said:

"When the people fear the government there is tyranny.

When the government fears the people there is liberty".

If we hope to maintain our independence, we cannot stop until government officials fear us. "We the Taxslaves" are the economic backbone of the country. Hopefully soon, we will be able to look back and say, "Mission accomplished". Our elected rulers understand that progressive politics is destructive by design – now it is our turn to destroy the political powers that work to strip our liberties. Taxpayers are being forced into proactive self-preservation. **We do not want to end up like the fallen empires that we read about in our history books.** Our political ruling class must realize that if things do not change, all out political revolution is not only possible, but it is probable.

Political uprisings of the past were a result of government recklessness and it will happen again if poisonous political practices continue to threaten "We the People".

The TEA Parties are simply American taxpayers trying to get the attention of their rulers. This is our attempt to tell them exactly what we want, and what we do not want. The problem is, they are not listening. When we exhaust all of our options and have no other recourse, **revolution is our only option.**

Our politicians no longer want to govern; they want to rule. They have made a mockery of our political process. The media has portrayed Tea Party activists as radical, white racists. We were mocked and attacked in the news for speaking out against Big Government. Change is indeed coming. Frustration is transforming into action. We know that sending letters and e-mail will not change our current path. Our political ruling class has attempted to shut us out of the political process.

Thomas Jefferson said, *"A little revolution is good from time to time"*.

The Tea Party revolts were not filled with reckless people, and they certainly were not violent. The Tea Parties represent organized self-defense. **This revolution will not be fought on the streets with bayonets; it will be waged at the voting booths on Election Day.** At a time when the states need to go to war with the Federal monster, state representatives are being bribed. Instead of fighting against the Federal Government for overstepping its well-defined boundaries, our state leaders are accepting payoffs in the form of Federal dollars for their districts in order to secure their re-election. If we all have a right to equal protection under the law, why are some of us taxed at a higher rate than others? Some people are flat out given money simply because they exist. Where is the equality and equal protection in these cases? Does "equal protection" apply to our earnings? Apparently it does not. It is time for the American Taxslaves to take back control if the government. We need representatives in office who truly are "Of the people, by the people and for the people" to protect us from all threats, foreign or domestic.

It is time to awaken from false dreams. We can no longer believe that the false prophets of government will be saviors to us.

Enslaving taxes have a negative impact on our lives. A disaster is on the way - our ship is sinking. If we plug the first visible leak, ten more pop up in other areas. If you take the pressure off of one leak, it will fall on another. We must rebuild the ship of liberty and restore its original glory. We must also find a new captain and a new crew that will navigate us home safely. **It is time to restore American Liberty as our founders intended it.**

America's founding was based on the principles of freedom and independence. **The birth of our American Nation was an experiment that set the soul of man free to discover and push the known limits of achievement and prosperity.** In the beginning, America was a piece of Heaven on Earth. Unfortunately it has turned into an economically imprisoning hell.

Today, too many Americans, both citizens and politicians, are working tirelessly to get more for themselves at the expense of others. This is a result of growing government influence on our lives. This behavior has led to a sense of entitlement that too many people in our society feel. Many Americans believe they deserve something just because someone else has it. This kind of thinking has transformed a free and independent society into a "dependent" and "expecting" group of babies that will throw tantrums if their demands are not met.

With each passing day we are subjected to people that preach about the inequalities that they have been subjected to. Americans are told that the "system" is designed to keep them down. Those who speak these words are the people who want their needs "provided for" at the expense of those who get up and work hard for what they earn. We continually hear debates and heated arguments about equality. **If we are truly "created equal" then why do some of us pay a greater percentage of our income simply because we work harder and try harder than others?** Some people gain measurable success while taking advantage of an opportunity. Through positive circumstances, hard work and a little luck, some Americans end up with more money and wealth than others. This is not evil - it is simply a result of sacrifice and hard work. Success is not guaranteed. Because we have hope we keep trying. Unfortunately, success is punished by a progressive tax structure that closely resembles legal extortion. We need to restore America back to a piece Heaven on Earth and break free from the captivity of economic enslavement. **It is once again time to catch the spirit of 1776 and fight for the opportunity to become a free and independent people once again.**

How is it that the priority of Americans is no longer individual liberty and freedom? Now, the focus has become economic equality. This has evolved from a quest for control and domination. The American Taxslaves must work to remove central planning (a euphemism for Big Government control) that is used to manage too many aspects of our individual lives. There is not a single person on this earth who will work harder than I will to create a better life better for myself. If we cast Big Government out of our lives we will be much better off as a country and as individuals. Americans have the ability to manage their own lives effectively without strong-armed intervention from government strangers. According to our "rulers" economic catastrophe is the perfect environment to rein in more government control. This can only lead to a decrease in personal liberties. Our government is saturated with unworthy men and women who seek to gain power at our expense. Since we repeatedly put them in office we are waterlogged in our own stupidity. Our present government does not respond to the economic anguish felt by the American Taxslaves. We simply want our "leaders" to stop spending us into slavery; we want the spending to stop. Our freedom is a blessing, a treasure that was discovered by men and women who changed the course of the modern world. We need to look upon our independence with respect and appreciation. Too many Americans have failed to show the proper appreciation for our freedom. We have given the duty of protecting our freedom to a government that is made up of unworthy servants of the people.

Instead of relentlessly protecting our independence, we hand over control to our rulers - with hope that they will do the right thing to secure and maintain it. We have placed too much trust in our political ruling class. The unfortunate consequence is that they have looked out for their own interests, not that of the American taxpayers. "We the People" cannot simply be "holders" of freedom; it is our duty as Americans to be "defenders" of freedom. We have all heard the plea, "Can't we all just get along"? The answer is no, we cannot "all just get along." Many Americans want to maintain their independence from Big Government while others prefer dependence on Big Government. Because of this disconnect, "We the People" can no longer "get along". **Why should we "get along" and accept the fact that we are subjected to the reign of our rulers.** Our elite political class has come to rule us, and control us. Our economic interests come second to theirs.

Our current politicians do not inspire bravery. Instead, they encourage us to rely on organized government to provide for our individual needs. Simply put, our rulers encourage cowardice.

The task of self-government is not something that can be set on autopilot.

Our nation will grow to be prosperous if each American works to become more self-reliant. This can only happen if we have a firm understanding of the proper role of government in our lives. Our rulers ask us to give up our freedom and our tax dollars in order to help them fix the problems that they create. They bail us out of man-made economic disasters using our own money. Politicians tell us, "Give us more control, we will do it for you". Our leaders do not encourage us to do what is necessary. Instead, they ask us to do what is easy. Nothing good has ever come from a body of political dependents. As a result, our rulers are in control and we have become Taxslaves. This is not a good tradeoff. We must cut the cord and re-learn the value of independence and personal responsibility.

Americans have empowered a political ruling class with the ability to exert dominion over us like subjects to a king. "We the People" must return to a mindset where we are responsible for our own actions and are ready to live with the consequences of our decisions.

Our elected politicians must be an honest check and balance between freedom and tyranny. Legislators should not be up for sale. Sadly, our politicians are for sale, their votes are on the auction block and as a result, our tax dollars are going to the highest bidder. America was intended to be a country of the people – not a monarchical structure with a political ruling class that exerts control over the people.

Some people believe that implementing term limits will provide the solution to this problem. Term limits will encourage our rulers to take more from us in a shorter period of time. It is time to overhaul our entire political power structure. We can achieve this by electing true conservative taxpayers to serve in public office.

We must put real people into office and let them do the things that real people do on a daily basis, things like balance budgets and re-introduce the concept of non-interference to government.

Our country can only be as good as the people who govern it. We are doing a terrible job choosing effective representatives to serve in office. Once elected, our politicians stop listening to us. This is our own fault because we keep putting them back into their seats of political privilege. When a politician does not do what he was put in office to do, we as taxpayers look the other way. As a result, we deserve everything that we get in return for our poor decisions. Now is the time for real change. In order to achieve this, we must take the training wheels off. A "government-funded" lifestyle does not build self-confidence - it encourages dependence. Taxslaves must work hard to empower themselves and reject the offer by government to do the things that we must do for ourselves. We need to get Big Government out of our way. These United American States will not continue to exist unless we begin producing products that will allow for American economic dominance in a growing competitive world.

The monster of government has become an un-tamed beast. Big Government has escaped from its cage and is too big to effectively control. In order to save ourselves from being consumed by this despotic beast, we must "put it down" like a dangerous wild animal. This can only happen at the voting booths.

Those of us that choose to fight have a bumpy road ahead of us. The bully is waiting in the schoolyard and it is three O'clock. Our goal is to leave school and get home in one piece. We know that we must first go outside and face the bully. We may not win the fight alone, but if enough people that have been bullied stick together, go outside, line up and face the bully head on, we will make it home safely. America has to make it back home – to the comfort of independence. The American Taxslaves must work together in achieving this goal.

The mercenaries of the Tax Apocalypse are gearing up and preparing for a political war. Prepare yourselves to withstand their assault. Our ammunition will be awareness and reason – this will be our only salvation from further political oppression and economic enslavement from the hands of our out of touch ruling class.

Americans are under the false illusion that the role of government is to act as caretakers for its citizens. Does it make you nervous to think that a government "big enough to give you everything you need" is also "big enough to take away everything you have"? In America, government does not create our rights. Our rights come directly from God. These rights are "endowed by our Creator". **Government does not create rights - dictators and rulers create rights.** The elected representatives of free men and women do not create rights because man-made rights can be confiscated and re-defined. Government must not direct the course of our lives - we must lead ourselves in the direction of our choice – within the clearly established laws of our nation – our Constitution. Government must once again begin to operate under the "consent of the governed" within the constraints set by our Constitution. Americans must stop ignoring the clear fact that our rulers are doing great damage to the Republic. American citizens can no longer pretend that Big Government has not taken control of all aspects of our lives – including our wallets. Taxpayers cannot ignore the obvious fact that we are heading down a dangerous "Road to Serfdom". We must stop pretending that the problem of despotic government does not exist and start working to solve it.

Many people have told me, "Watch out because government bites". Well if that is true, then Americans need to "bite back"! I know that I cannot do this alone, so please, come join me.

The American Taxslaves must sharpen their teeth and pierce the skin of Big Government. Point your finger in the face of Big Government and shout, "Don't tread on us"!

I refuse to fund more wasteful government projects because I detest forcibly imposed change. **I refuse to sit back quietly and watch as our rulers "fundamentally transform" these United States".**

We must demand that our elected representatives do what they were put in office to do - uphold the Constitution of the United States and protect the rights given to us by our Creator. The various levels and branches of our government have a responsibility to protect our freedoms, not limit them.

Americans are living in a historical political moment in time. We are faced with a difficult choice. We can either stay on the same path of destruction that other fallen empires chose in the past, or we can choose the path of personal responsibility, independence and freedom. Most people are not confident enough to know that we do not need government to do things for us. Real change will come when "We the People" assume responsibility for effectively governing our own lives.

Only a free and independent body of citizens can embrace responsibility. Dependents need to be told what to do. Mostly every human on this planet wants the safe feeling that someone else has the answers. I refuse to follow someone else's lead. A body of free and independent people will choose self-governance before they allow a ruling class to exert control over them. Political comfort is dangerous because it can leave us dependant on someone else for our survival – as a result we become slaves to the demands of our governing class. Free men control their own lives – they do not delegate the responsibility to anyone else. Americans must work hard and strip the political power from our political "masters". Only then will we achieve confidence, self-worth and independence. Personal responsibility will set us free from tyranny of any kind. Self-reliance is the key ingredient in the battle to end our dependence on Big Government. **Americans must learn how to become self-reliant so that we can once again execute mastery over our own lives.** Why allow some faceless bureaucrat to govern the course of your life? Real independence comes from understanding the fact that we can take care of ourselves. As free Americans, we must direct the course of our own lives. We are in the driver's seat and it is within our ability to get back on the road to liberty, freedom, and individual responsibility. Not a single corporation or business is "too big to fail". Failure is good because it makes us stronger, self-reliant and more capable of self-governing.

The American people have lost their sense of political wisdom. Our governing process has become something that it was never intended to be - a popularity contest backed by big money and uncontrolled political "influence". America has become a society of people who are comfortable. As a result of this, "We the People" have failed to hold our elected leaders accountable for their destructive actions.

America belongs to the "We the People" – so lets start acting like stockholders in freedom and independence. As citizens, each of us is a CEO of American liberty. Now we must make an executive decision to either sink or swim and keep this country afloat so that we can sail off to a better and more prosperous future.

Taxpayers have become Economically Enslaved Tax Peasants

Can I tell you a secret? We are not as free as we think we are – American taxpayers have become Taxslaves to a lawless political ruling class.

We are watching the systematic dismantling of the American political system. We are witnesses to the economic genocide of the American Taxslaves.

The laws of economics are simple. Economic principles apply to government in the same method that they apply to our personal lives. If you do not have money, you cannot spend it. If you spend money that you do not have (by borrowing) you cannot push the bill off onto someone else to pay. The average American does not manage their financial resources like a teenager that has mom and dad to bail them out – but our politicians do. Taxpaying Americans must live within their means and effectively manage their own financial resources. Americans are in a quest for political and economic survival. Our politicians act like spoiled little children. Politicians treat the American Taxslaves like rich parents.

Our rulers fail to consider that taxpayers are mothers and fathers looking to take care of their own children. Americans do not want to provide for government employees and social program recipients. Taxpayers fund the salaries, pensions and benefits for most of the federal, state, county, and city employees. As taxpayers, we need to take care of ourselves and tend our own homes. I do not water my neighbor's garden - I take care of my own garden because I want my flowers to grow. If I choose to, I can lend a helping hand to a neighbor - but is must be my choice, not my duty. Let me make it very clear, - helping others should be a choice, not a duty imposed on us by our government. Most Americans will "give back to their communities" once members of their communities stop taking from them by way of wealth redistribution. It is not up to me - as a free man - to address the economic needs of others before addressing my own economic needs first. This false compassion is Tax Slavery in disguise.

Members of American society that do not pay taxes should not have a say in regard to how the hard earned tax dollars of the productive members are spent. Until members of a community become contributing taxpayers, they should not have a say in the financial affairs of their community. The ability to vote on city and school budgets should be a privilege that is earned by contributing to the services needed to fuel your local community.

Do you think it is fair that a person who does not contribute to his or her community is allowed to reap the benefits of the work that another person does?

The American tax system has become perverted; distorted by a ruling class that seeks to re-distribute our earned income to those who trade their votes in return for handouts. One portion of our society has become dependent on another portion. Our government facilitates this perversion of the American social order. **If you do not own a home, you should not have input in how homeowner property tax dollars are spent. We cannot allow one group of voters to vote themselves additional perks and services at the expense of the Taxpaying portion of our communities – The American Taxslaves.** We must get rid of the political rhetoric and the feel-good speeches that make us all feel warm and fuzzy inside. Speeches that are full of "hope" and "false compassion" can only get us so far. Somebody has to pay for the political promises of candidates and elected officials. **I refuse to let my neighbor tell me how to spend what I earn.** Essentially, this is what is happens when we allow people to vote themselves a free ride. Our property taxes are rising at an unprecedented rate because we have too many people in our communities that do not own property but yet still have the ability to vote on school and city budgets. This is more in-line with Socialism, not Americanism. The American tax system has been perverted. **We must restore order and balance to our**

local communities. The mending process will begin when we fight to reform voter requirements. We need to have open debates and encourage honest discussions about the issues that are destroying our communities. Stand up to your mayor, stand up to your city council, stand up to your elected officials and loudly proclaim, "Stand on the side of the Taxslaves or step aside".

In a democracy, citizens are subjected to majority rule. This is in direct opposition to a constitutional republic. What will happen if the majority of voters become tax consumers and demand that they want someone else to take care of their needs? What happens when 51 percent of the people find out that they can "live" off of the other 49 percent of the people? This means that the taxpayers will essentially become slaves to the wants and needs of the many. We can combat this injustice by restoring the principles of true freedom - a true constitutional republic where the majority cannot vote away the rights of the minority.

What would happen if we put a 10% cap on the income tax or eliminate it fully and explore the "Fair Tax"- a flat consumption based tax? It is time to rearrange the furniture in Washington, but first we must re-arrange the furniture in our own homes.

The American Taxslaves have been stripped of their ability to make individual choices in regard to how their earned income is spent. Thanks to Uncle Sam, we keep less and less of our earnings.

Big Government is robbing the Bank of the Taxpayers.

We need to return government back to the proper owners – the American people. "We the People" own this government. So, let's enforce the clearly defined rules of operation. It is time to restore the founding principles that served as the foundation of American prosperity. We must resist the temptation to accept our current system of despotic government control. Our foundation is firm, but the rampant corruption in our governing process must be abolished. Once we shed our blind loyalty to Big Government, we will finally begin our journey towards freedom with an untainted state of a mind. It is time to get rid of our loyalty to Republicans and Democrats. Train your mind to see through the Judas-like false prophets and look past the political games. We have been escorted down the road to dependence. It is now time to dispose of the "R" and the "D" so that we can get back on the track of self-government as our founders intended. We are lucky that the founding fathers had the foresight to leave us a "trail of breadcrumbs" so that if we ever deviated from our path, we still had the ability to find our way back to freedom and independence. Our Constitution is the true home of liberty. Knowledge, commitment and hard work are the guiding lights that will lead us home safely.

A resurrection of America's original purpose, freedom from tyranny, is what will save our American Republic.

Political party loyalty and charming politicians will not be saviors to the American people. Our political class has poisoned America. Our journey will begin when we start looking to the men who abolished tyranny from the shores of these United States. Our courage and unbreakable revolutionary spirit are the only reasons why we are here today living in the greatest Republic that the world has ever seen. Americans must once again show great respect, honor and gratitude for the men and women who are responsible for creating these United States.

At the time of their resistance, our founders had no idea what their impact on the world would be. They simply did what they felt was right. These men were heroes. They were men of integrity and honor. Each day of my life I wake up - infused with the hope that I can be half the man that any one of them proved to be.

"I have sworn upon the altar of God, eternal hostility against every form of tyranny over the mind of man".

-Thomas Jefferson

A free body of people can only remain free if they understand what freedom is - and how to maintain it. Once the mind of a man is awakened he will remain free and independent forever – regardless of any physical captivity he may be subjected to. But, if you paralyze the mind of a man it will be easy to enslave him. Physical restraints are not necessary to hold men captive because control over the minds of men is the easiest way to keep them in a state of subservience.

Most Americans do not fully appreciate and show reverence for their unique history. John Locke wrote about the idea of government operating under the "consent of the governed". This idea was an important principle in the America's liberation from Great Britain. Locke frequently wrote about the principles of "Natural Law". This was prevalent in the minds of America's founding fathers when they wrote the following:

"We hold these truths to be self-evident, that all men are created equal, that they are endowed by their Creator with certain unalienable Rights, that among these are Life, Liberty and the pursuit of Happiness. — That to secure these rights, Governments are instituted among Men, deriving their just powers from the consent of the governed, — That whenever any Form of Government becomes destructive of these ends, it is the Right of the People to alter or to abolish it, and to institute new Government...."

This is a frightening and powerful idea, which requires bravery, knowledge, wisdom and patience to enforce.

It is perhaps the greatest of all of our founders' writings.

The current system of politically enforced economic servitude must be erased from American shores. We need to elect public servants who are not afraid to make difficult decisions and enforce the legislative change that we desperately need. Working to change the political power structure will be extremely difficult. Powerful special interest groups with endless financial resource stand in our way. These groups fund campaigns and provide huge monetary contributions to the candidates who act as their indentured servants. Political puppets vote in favor of the legislation that will best serve their big "special interest" masters.

Political action committees, public employee unions, and lobbying groups donate more to political campaigns than the average American worker will ever earn in a lifetime. Do not allow yourselves to submit to their influence at election time. Be a free man, not a slave. Open your mind and focus on the work that must be done. Work to liberate the Taxslaves. Have you ever wondered why political action groups spend so much money to get people elected to office? The reason is simple: these people benefit at the expense of the American taxpayers.

Criminals, both inside and outside of government, have abused our political system. We are witnessing the systematic attempt to abandon our Constitutionally limited government. Both political parties, Republicans and Democrats, are guilty of exploiting the American Taxslaves. Both parties have abandoned us. Republicans and Democrats are both big spenders that are in favor of growing the size of government bigger and bigger. The purpose of serving in office must not be to get re-elected. Public servants must work to do what is right for American freedom. "We the People" must force them to protect the Constitution and preserve the liberties of the people. After all, we are the cornerstone and foundation of our Republic. Politicians must be forced to serve their purpose then get out of our way!

Something is wrong with the American people these days. Too many of us sit back and allow dishonest rulers to direct the course of our lives. Our political class is dishonest. The words they say may make sense, but their actions and the things they do prove that they are only hungry for control. **Both Democrats and Republicans have lost touch with the American people.** We cannot give a ruling class this much power and control over our lives. Roughly half of the taxpaying Americans work year goes to some level of government to provide services that we either do not need or can provide better for ourselves. We need to work on reducing the amount of government employees that we are "forced" to provide for. Everyone on a government payroll must understand that each paycheck they get comes from a taxpaying member of the public sector. Government employees must open their eyes and recognize that each pay-raise, benefit increase and pension package is funded on the backs of the private sector Taxslaves. We need to eliminate the public employee unions and strip their ability to negotiate ironclad contracts that ensure raises, pensions and benefits for their members year after year with no end in sight. This economic burden is strapped to the back of the Taxslaves just like the Cross Jesus was forced to carry. Unfortunately, we will not forgive their sins.

Americans have become indentured servants. We are forced to pay for the sweetheart deals of civil servants and public employee unions. Taxpayers that earn a living in the private sector struggle with tax hike after tax hike. Public employees and social program recipients are the people who benefit the most from the hard work and sacrifice of regular American Taxslaves.

Government employee unions and complicit politicians are ruining this country! They trade votes for favorable legislation.

We need to restore America back to the "Land of Opportunity". Tax cuts will lead to economic prosperity. This will happen if we choose to cut the size of government and drastically reduce spending.

Power is created through dependence. If you need a person or group for help, your economic survival or your happiness, you are essentially a slave to their demands. Politicians will exert mastery over you if you rely on them for your existence. If this is the case, you have been effectively enslaved. They can and will dominate every aspect of your life. "We the People" need to take control of our political process. **Our public servants are not leaders – they are rulers.** The ultimate goal of our political ruling class is control over the American Taxslaves.

I dare you to answer this question "Do you trust any level of your own government."? The answer is no.

Government has become a big, faceless entity with front men who sell us false compassion and manufactured sincerity. Government has become a broker of greed. We must fight to win our economic independence from these rulers and conquer the false prophets who want dominion over us for their own prosperity.

American citizens must work together to institute real change. We must put the actions of our elected rulers on display for everyone to see. Teach others to see through the smiling faces, scams and gimmicks that have allowed the problem of Big Government to continue. Our current political class is giving away our income faster than we can earn it. Politicians cost us more than they provide for us. Our rulers are architects of deception; they are the catalyst of economic destruction. American taxpayers must take care their own economic needs before they take care of the economic needs of their neighbors. We cannot offer help to others until we have a firm, solid foundation to work from. It is time for Big Government to pack it's bags and get out of our lives.

A despotic ruling class is longer welcome in American politics.

It is time for the American Taxslaves to do the work that is required to live free from economic enslavement. As free American citizens we will provide for our own needs in a manner that is smarter, cheaper and better than the politicians do. One intended purpose of big organized government was to provide services better, faster and cheaper than the private sector. Unfortunately for the American Taxslaves, the system of Big Government has failed. Privatizing certain services will be more cost effective for the taxpaying portion of our communities. American citizens must start to do things on their own instead of looking to government for a handout. Give the free market a chance to operate without the burden of Big Government.

American taxpayers in search of relief must begin to endorse constitutionally minded candidates who run for public office. In order to be free, we must understand how self-government was intended to function. We need to gain a firm grasp on political party ideology and how it relates to the Constitution. Public officials must enforce protection of the rights that are "endowed by our Creator". We must understand how the structure of a free and self-governing society works if we are going to learn how to operate within the framework of our Constitutional Republic. Go read the Constitution, the Declaration of Independence and the Bill of Rights – I bet you have not read these since high school. I promise, you will be surprised to see how your understanding of these documents has changed since you read them in high school. The ability to self-govern is within our ability. Our founders did it, so why can't we do it? We simply need to understand the intended purpose of our government if we plan to fix it.

America is in desperate need of people who want to serve - not people who want to rule and conquer. Our elected officials continue to ignore the demands of the Taxslaves. A great deal of work is needed. Thankfully, each day, more and more of us are willing to perform it. Many brave Americans taxpayers are prepared to stand on the front lines ready to rise up and take back control of their government. "We the People" must once again become leaders. **It is our duty to cast out the rulers who have hijacked our Republic.** Even if you are not the brightest, smartest, or most charismatic, you can fulfill your obligation to fight for your right to self-govern. **Make an appeal to the better angels in your nature, and then come join us on the front line in this new War for American Independence.** It is time for us to rise to the challenge of self-government. We cannot wait for someone else to do it for us.

Cowards bow down to a ruling class, slaves bow down before a master, free men will fight to the end before they kneel to a king

The American taxpayers have been reduced to economically imprisoned Taxslaves. Free people keep what they earn - slaves are forced to give the product of their labor to a master. It is my hope that one day we will put an end to the lies, manipulation and deception that has become the basis of our political system. A life lived free from despotism and economic enslavement is the only life worth living.

America is a Constitutional Republic. This nation was never intended to be a "majority rule" democracy. In a democracy the minority is subject to the tyranny of the majority. The American people have lost focus on the American concept of liberty. This is why we need voter reform. Can you honestly tell me that everyone you know who votes is well informed? Do most American citizens understand the differences between the political policies being debated? Or, do Americans just react to that warm, fuzzy feeling that consumes them when a polished and charismatic candidate speaks? I think it is safe to assume that most people just say, "I like him, he's just like me, he's one of us, I am going to go out and vote for him". In our last presidential election the country - myself included, got so caught up in the "hope" and "change" messages that we could not see what was coming. We quickly realized that our elected officials are not "just like us". Obama for example, was a senator that made millions of dollars from the books that he wrote. He is not like most hard-working, over-taxed, struggling Americans – he is a wealthy man of privilege. Obama, his administration, and those that "serve" with him are not like most American taxpayers. Our "leaders" are out of touch men and women of privilege who play on our fears and create a false sense of compassion. By expanding the federal budget and exponentially increasing the size of government, our rulers have exposed themselves. What happened to the campaign promise of an open and transparent government? In regard to the "Health Care Bill" (HR 3200), House Speaker Nancy Pelosi said, ***"We need to pass the bill so that you can find out what is in it".*** Shame on us – we were fooled. Thankfully it has only made us stronger and more aware. A wolf in sheep's clothing has stealthily entered our homes. **Unfortunately, we have to deal with the political mess we've made. But, make no mistake; we are prepared and ready to protect our American Republic from any future threat.**

It is our duty to change the course of American politics. We will achieve our independence the good old-fashioned way – through revolution. We can restore the principles of a constitutionally limited republic through political activism. Politicians will only make things worse - they cannot fix things. Ronald Reagan said, *"Government is not the solution to the problem, government is the problem".* Reagan also noted that *"As government expands liberty contracts".* Our current system of economically authoritarian government is deteriorating our nation and it's founding principles. I love my neighbors, my neighborhood and my community, and as a result I want to free the Taxslaves from the economic shackles that hold them captive. I am ready to shatter the curse of dependence on Big Government. Politicians will not resolve the crisis because they are the problem. Americans must embrace interaction with their elected officials. The relationship between those that govern and "the governed" must be based on trust and confidence. Only when we begin to look after each other, will we will be able to find a solution to our problem. The American people are the solution - not politicians.

We are victims of a political disaster that we have permitted to happen. Government does not create economically sensible programs and services - it destroys them. Government cannot create jobs that help the economy. Politicians can create laws that make things legal or illegal and give tax breaks to corporations that create products that help our economy. But, in most cases government legally confiscates wealth from corporations that would otherwise be allocated to create more jobs. American production industries are too entrenched in unionization. As a result of restrictive corporate taxes and union costs, American manufacturing industries have fled our shores like the retreating tyrants of the British Empire. Wake up Taxslaves - it is time to fight for your political and economic independence – so keep your political "guns" loaded. Our government is forcing wasteful social programs upon us. Social programs work more effectively in theory than they do in the real world. Big Government does not work effectively at a manageable cost to taxpayers. Taxpayers end up paying a government employee's salary, pension and benefits forever. As well, we pay for the individual that replaces them. As taxpayers, we pay this while we are still paying for the first retiree. It does not take a genius to see just how much of our money is wasted. This process is repeated over and over again. The cost of government continues to increase and, as a result, depletes the wealth of the taxpaying portion of our nation. The American Taxslaves are left to fund the lives of as many as four people (3 retirees and 1 active government employee) for the same government job.

This type of political and economic malpractice is causing our economic system to collapse. Public employee unions are the biggest cause of the enslaving tax burden forced upon the American Taxslaves.

Every check that a government cuts to one of its employees - for salary, benefits or pension - is a dollar that has been legally confiscated from a productive member of American society. Each dollar government spends is a dollar that has been extorted from an American Taxslave. Government spends a huge amount of money, and as a result, it takes an abundance of wealth away from the American citizens. We do not need more politicians to find "solutions" to problems that they are responsible for creating in the first place. We do not need to create more government departments to figure out ways to confiscate more of our hard earned tax dollars. My message is this: Leave us alone. Leave me alone - leave my pockets alone, leave my property and my income alone. If I make more money than my neighbor, maybe it is because I have sacrificed and worked hard to achieve moderate prosperity. Each of us must look out for our own financial well-being – not that of our neighbors. **I do not get up and go to work for government, government employees or the tax-consuming portion of society.** My government works for me. I work to be the best that I can be and have the best of what I can afford. I do not expect someone else to pay my way. We will be fine if we are left alone to secure economic stability for our own interests.

Government is getting so big because politicians are doing so many things they are not permitted to do that they cannot even do the things that they were put into office to do. Government does not earn money – it confiscates it. As a result, politicians are the ultimate gangsters.

Federal, State and Local government spending is out of control. This is due in part to public employee unions. We need to embrace major pension reform. Taxpayers must reconnect with the message of our founding fathers and scale back our current economically oppressive government. **Generous public employee union contracts are quickly putting an end to American prosperity!** The politically induced "free rides" must come to an end. Ambition and hard work must outweigh entitlements and handouts.

We must liberate the working class, liberate businesses, and liberate the American Tax Slaves. Our political ruling class has become a destroyer of wealth and opportunity.

Our leaders are not "uniters"; they have become "dividers".

Our government has been set up to make us feel small and irrelevant. Once we realize that we are not irrelevant, we can realize our power as individual sovereigns. "We the People" can change our political system if we put in the work to do it. We are not small and we are not unimportant. If we stand united, the American Taxslaves can bring about the necessary changes in government. We are closer to independence now than we have been at any point in modern history.

President Obama expressed his desire to "fundamentally transform" America – why? The truth is this; we must start by changing our minds and embracing independence – not dependence. We must transform our communities from un-involved to politically involved. When we do this, we will see these United States return to prosperity. It is within our power to change anything we want to change, so do not let politicians convince you that there is nothing we do about the tyrannical tax enslavement. If a system was put in place by politics, then "We the People" can undo it. Political party association is of no consequence. Both Republicans and Democrats are guilty of economically enslaving the American taxpayers. Dirty political fingerprints are all over the lawmaking political process that has been used to strip "We the People" of the power to govern the course of our own lives. Government has grown much too powerful on all levels - local, state and federal level. Big Government has done unforgivable damage to the legacy of this American Nation. Extreme damage has been done to our great Republic. Our Constitution has been re-translated and in many cases circumvented in order to fit the political agenda of our rulers.

Our unfit leaders in Washington have imposed an unimaginable transfer of wealth on the taxpaying portion of America. Our rulers legally confiscate the earned economic property of those that produce and hand it out to those that do not produce. This Socialist agenda is a severe threat to the liberties of all American citizens.

It is impossible for a governing body to tax citizens into greater economic prosperity. Private industry and businesses create wealth - not government. Big Government and individual liberty cannot co-exist in a free society. Independence and subservience to government cannot coexist in a Republic. American taxpayers have a decision to make – keep the product of your labor or give it away. Fight the battle for economic independence or give in to the demands of your rulers. Every action has an equal and opposite reaction. So, when government on every level confiscates money from taxpayers, it causes the equal and opposite reaction - taxpayers keep less of what they work to gain. This forces taxpayers to do more with less.

Our current un-constitutional system of wealth-redistribution allows government dependents to prosper through the confiscated earnings of the American Taxslaves. **American Taxpayers are forced to "do more with less" so that Big Government can "do less with more".**

If we want to jumpstart production and prosperity, we need to cut the cost of doing business here in America. This will allow American businesses to be competitive in the important production industries. High business taxes have caused immeasurable damage to the American economy.

Hostile financial constraints on businesses have paralyzed the American workforce while overseas markets have thrived. Change is indeed needed – it will start with us.

We are subjected to a political ruling class that shows contempt for the true economic backbone of this country - the American Taxslaves.

Politicians on all levels claim that they are open to suggestions. They say, "Give us suggestions that will help us help you". I have a suggestion for them, it is very simple; **leave town**! American taxpayers must secure seats in political office. **It is time to force change by the strength of our own hands and minds**. It is time for action – political action. This is our moment in history and we cannot let it pass us by. It is time to re-establish a true Constitutional Republic. **Our rights are "Endowed by our Creator ", not our government, and especially not our political ruling class – so start behaving like it.**

We are at a very important moment in American history. The most terrifying of all of our threats comes from inside of our own borders.

Make your choice - independence, freedom, and prosperity, or, dependence, economic enslavement and failure. I am ready to fight for my independence. Are you?

Our rulers have constructed a wall

I am still fairly young, but I can still remember, just as many Americans can too, the fall of Communism. I can remember over twenty years ago, when the former Soviet Union crumbled under the weight of its own wickedness.

I can still hear the words of Ronald Reagan echo in my ears:

"Mr. Gorbachev, tear town this wall".

People danced in the streets and celebrated throughout the world as they watched the fall of Communism - when the totalitarian rule of Eastern Europe was dragged to its knees.

At that moment, not only Americans, but also, people across the world rejoiced.

I was so proud to be an American that day. America was a symbol of all that was good in the world. Today, just as on that day, I am proud to be an American. The Berlin Wall, which represented the world's symbol of oppression and tyranny, was torn down, by the hands of the people who were oppressed by it's threatening image and what it represented.

But now, here in America, twenty years later - our political ruling class has constructed a wall of their own. It is a wall between our political class and the American people.

Our society has been split into two divisions - Taxpayers and Tax Consumers. A new Cold War is being fought – between dependents on Big Government, and those who embrace personal responsibility and independence.

We have an opportunity to make sure that, in a generation from now, we can look back and tell our children and grandchildren about what we did – how we fought, and won the Second American Revolution. We can tell them about how we freed the American Taxslaves and won our independence back from Big Government. We will be able to tell our children **about the time when OUR WALL CAME CRUMBLING DOWN!**

Ignite inside yourself a flame, one that burns with the desire to govern the course of your own life

There is a clear disconnect between the ruling class and the taxpaying people. While the debate between political ideologies goes on, the American Taxslaves are suffering. Americans must put an end the argument and focus on restoring true freedom, liberty and American prosperity. We must work hard to restore a constitutionally limited government. We must remember the words of Henry David Thoreau, *"Government is best which governs least"*. Americans must gain a clear understanding of what freedom really is. American citizens must work tirelessly to produce the most capable elected leaders from our communities. We must not allow our legislators to pass reckless and un-affordable bills. The wasteful cost of Big Government has proven that our current politicians are incapable of leading us to economic prosperity. This is why "We the People" must stop looking to government to do things for us. We must work to achieve things on our own. Each physically able American citizen is capable of achieving relative prosperity.

The American Taxslaves must work hard to gain legislative power and implement policies that will work to the benefit of the taxpaying portion of society. Government cannot continue to enhance benefits for the tax-consuming politicians, public employees and social program recipients. **Political contamination has led to a massive decline in many American communities. The American political system has been infected with**

the virus of Big Government. We must implement policies that are in-line with the best interests of the hard working American Taxslaves. Our generation does not understand the value of American independence and the extreme sacrifices that previous generations made to secure it. Freedom and economic independence have no price tag. American taxpayers are the economic backbone of this country; therefore we must work to maintain it.

Regular American men and women must hit the political scene like a ray of light shining through the cold winter of Big Government. Freedom, independence and personal accountability are once again in bloom. Now is the time to start planting the seeds of liberty and prosperity.

The Americans Taxslaves are ready to reclaim their economic independence.

It is time to collect all of the garbage in government, bag it up and leave it outside on the curb for the garbage men to take away. **It is time to clean up our government. My voice is simply an echo of the millions and millions of taxpayers across this country that represent the beginning of our rulers' fall from grace.**

Politicians who are unable to stand on the side of the American taxpayers need to step aside and let real patriots get things done. If they cannot do their job, we the Taxslaves will do it for them.

Passionate and patriotic Americans are on the rise in the tens of millions. Our oppressive rulers cannot suppress an uprising of this magnitude. We sit quietly, but our blood is boiling. In time, our frustration and passion will erupt into a full-blown political revolution. The American Taxslaves will explode, and when that happens, our political class will feel the earth shake under their feet. The rulers will feel our wrath. They will hear our voices, and when this happens there will be nothing that can help them. We are going to take back control of our own lives. We will not trust our elected leaders to fix things; they have failed us over and over again. We must now rely on ourselves to restore the principles upon which these United States were established.

History is in the making. Our time in history will be remembered as America's re-birth. Each one of us must do our part to prevent a hostile ruling class from succeeding in their quest for dominance and control over us. **Our generation will be remembered as the generation that resuscitates American freedom, independence and personal**

accountability, or, as the generation that seals the decline of our American Republic. I know what I want the pages of my time in history to say. We are our own government - regular men and women who believe in a constitutionally limited republic that is "Of the people, by the people and for the people".

Americans must understand that private property, free enterprise, and firearms are all as essential to maintain our independence.

Deception and manipulation are deep rooted in our political process. Lies are the breeding ground for political poison. Politics is rooted in evil because it is a quest for power and control over the lives of men. Campaigns are built on deception and administrations manipulate the citizens to maintain control over the governing process. As a result, American taxpayers have become economically enslaved Tax Peasants. We can only shield ourselves from lies with knowledge and understanding of what self-government truly is. Our despotic ruling class has abandoned "We the Taxslaves", and in the process they have abandoned the American experiment of liberty. We must take it back.

I am not here to tell you that I can fix things. I am here because I need help. I need your help. Together, "We the People" can bring about the real change that is desperately needed in America. The taxpayers and the people out on the street taking part in the true TEA Party movements are the new revolutionaries that will save our American Republic. We are our only hope for change - not politicians. **A restoration of our American Republic starts with you.**

We must remember, "a house divided cannot stand".

Ignite inside yourself a flame, one that burns with the desire to govern the course of your own life....
We are the keepers of the flame that represents liberty and freedom, that of which we will flourish and conquer the tyrants of oppression and tyranny!
Big Government is the enemy of liberty, now go fight for your independence...
A great political awakening is upon us...
America must once again be baptized in the Fire of Liberty.

Conclusion:

A spirit is haunting these United American States…
A revolutionary spirit has infected the soul of America…
This rebellious uprising is now haunting the unholy political
alliances of our ruling class…

We are here to take back control of our government…
The question is not who is going to let us do it…
The question is…
Who is going to stop us?

You are the American Dream!

TAXSLAVES UNITE.